Praise for *Beyond the Building*

"If you're in CRE, whether you're starting out or an experienced CRE professional, this book will be fun, inspiring, and quite the learning tool."

—Scott C. Alper, President and CIO, Witkoff

"The book goes past the numbers and teaches people how to think and plan. The math part is easy; success starts with planning a path first."

—Mark Finerman, CEO, LoanCore Capital, LLC

"A powerful read for a young entrepreneur or seasoned real estate operator looking for a competitive advantage."

—Alex Rodriguez, Chairman and CEO, A-Rod Corp

"Rob Finlay has put together a great 'leadership road map' for anyone looking to grow and enhance their commercial real estate business."

—Joe Lubeck, Founder and CEO, American Landmark Apartments

BEYOND
THE
BUILDING

BEYOND THE BUILDING

HOW TO USE INNOVATION TO CREATE AND GROW YOUR COMMERCIAL REAL ESTATE PORTFOLIO

ROB FINLAY

GREENLEAF
BOOK GROUP PRESS

Published by Greenleaf Book Group Press
Austin, Texas
www.gbgpress.com

Distributed by Greenleaf Book Group

For ordering information or special discounts for bulk purchases, please contact Greenleaf Book Group at PO Box 91869, Austin, TX 78709, 512.891.6100.

Design and composition by Greenleaf Book Group and Sheila Parr
Cover design by Greenleaf Book Group and Sheila Parr
Author photo credit: Bryan Bazemore

Publisher's Cataloging-in-Publication data is available.

Hardcover ISBN: 979-8-88645-106-1

Paperback ISBN: 978-1-63299-706-7

eBook ISBN: 979-8-88645-108-5

Audiobook ISBN: 979-8-88645-107-8

To offset the number of trees consumed in the printing of our books, Greenleaf donates a portion of the proceeds from each printing to the Arbor Day Foundation. Greenleaf Book Group has replaced over 50,000 trees since 2007.

Printed in the United States of America on acid-free paper

23 24 25 26 27 28 29 30   10 9 8 7 6 5 4 3 2 1

First Edition

This book is dedicated to my parents, Chris and Carroll;
my kids, RJ, Maggie, Morgan, and Christa;
and my loving wife, Aynsley,
without whom this book would not exist.

Contents

Introduction

I'VE BEEN IN COMMERCIAL real estate (CRE) my entire life. My whole family—my late grandfather, my parents, and my brother—is or was in CRE. Growing up, even family vacations involved looking at real estate. It's all I've ever known. What I learned growing up in New Hampshire, and working in CRE ever since then, enabled me to create multiple businesses in the CRE space worth hundreds of millions of dollars. I got a boost because CRE was in my blood, but that doesn't mean it was easy. I had to learn many lessons the hard way. I wrote this book to make CRE easier for you than it was for me.

This book is for CRE operators and investors. It's for those with a lifetime of experience as well as those just getting started. I'll tell you what I've seen that works and what doesn't. I'll share what I learned from my front-row seat as I watched how the best CRE firms operate. Most importantly, I'll share what I know about innovation, technology, and data in CRE, because these forces are rapidly changing the industry. The next 50 years of CRE won't look like the last 50, and if you don't see beyond the building, you're going to get left behind.

AN EARLY START

When you grow up in a family business, you get to do every job in that business. Since my family's business was CRE, that means I cleaned buildings and toilets. I put up signs on buildings. I leased space, was a site superintendent, represented deals in planning board meetings, secured financing for projects, managed properties, and raised equity for deals—all before I was 25.

Another fact about growing up in a family business is that it's easy to take the experience for granted. For that reason, as soon as I could, I tried to get out of CRE. I felt like I had done it all, and I wanted something different. After I graduated from New Hampshire College (now Southern New Hampshire University), I found breaking out of CRE harder than I expected.

The first job I landed was working for Midlantic National Bank in New Jersey, as an analyst for Tom Hyland, who now handles commercial lending for PNC Bank in the Northeast. This was in 1992, right when the Resolution Trust Corporation (RTC) was dealing with the collapse of hundreds of banks nationwide. RTC's task was selling off the properties the defunct banks owned.

Because I already had experience with real estate, what other new college graduates didn't know was second nature to me. I rose quickly in the ranks, received valuable training, and learned the language of banking and finance. My job was to sell properties our bank had picked up, but by doing my job, I eventually worked myself out of it. At that point, I decided to take what I had learned back to New Hampshire, to the family business.

Like many 20-somethings, I thought I knew it all. After all, I had been to college and was already successful in my career. I felt I should be running the family business. My dad didn't agree. I ended up working on a New Hampshire construction site in the dead of winter. This certainly wasn't the life I wanted, and I began looking for something new.

WALL STREET-BOUND

I had always fantasized about working on Wall Street, in either mergers and acquisitions or trading, so in 1996 I applied for my dream job at Lehman Brothers. I was thrilled when I received an offer, but once again, I couldn't escape the world of CRE. Lehman Brothers offered me a job—not in mergers or acquisitions, nor in trading, but in real estate. It was exactly what I did *not* want to do. CRE loans were booming, and Lehman needed people with my expertise.

I took the job, but working at Lehman was nothing like the glamorous job I'd imagined. Each workday, I rode the elevator to the fourth floor of the World Financial Center. I went straight to my desk, which was located in what looked like a supply closet and was occupied by seven other guys. From morning until night, except for smoke breaks with Edmund Moy, I underwrote deals. I was what today would be called an acquisitions analyst, crunching numbers 24/7. It was more monotonous than anything.

In addition, for the first few months I worked at Lehman Brothers in New York, I lived in New Hampshire. This meant I left home each Monday morning at 4:00 a.m. and drove four hours to work. I slept on my buddy's futon during the week and then drove back to New Hampshire Friday night, getting in at around 11:00 p.m. Although I soon moved to New York, perhaps this added to my feeling that Lehman Brothers wasn't the place for me long term. After six months at Lehman Brothers, an opportunity came up to work at Credit Suisse First Boston (CSFB), and I jumped at it.

In 1998, I walked into the lobby of the New York headquarters of CSFB for my first day on the job. I felt completely out of place. Less than a year earlier, I had been working in construction. I was just a kid from rural New Hampshire. Everyone around me seemed to have an MBA from Wharton or another Ivy League school, whereas I had an undergraduate degree from a school no one had heard of. However, I knew commercial real estate inside and out, and that's what landed me the new job in the Flatiron District of Manhattan.

At CSFB, I was surrounded by CRE celebrities—among them Andy Stone, now of Petra Capital Management; Brian Harris, who later founded Ladder Capital; Mark Finerman, who runs LoanCore Capital; and Greta Guggenheim, who ran TPG Real Estate Finance Trust until her retirement. These individuals became superstars because they found ways to differentiate themselves within the CRE industry. I recognized that, in order to be successful, to get to that next level, that next opportunity, I, too, had to set myself apart. I found I had just two options: Either I needed to spot opportunities before others did, or I had to take risks others wouldn't take. I chose to do both.

I worked hard to study patterns and trends and make connections between events that others might not spot. This enabled me to find opportunities I knew were safe but that others thought were risky. I chose to dive in where many others wouldn't dip their toe. I loved the work I was doing and the people I worked with.

Unfortunately, although what we were doing at CSFB was impressive, the bank wasn't comfortable with the risks we were taking, and most of the department was let go. As we sat in a wide-open room, one by one we heard our names called by a guy in a suit. Finally, I heard, "Finlay, Rob. Grab your wallet, take out your company ID, and grab your jacket. Everything else stays on your desk, and we'll ship it to you." Just like that, I and many others were shown the door.

The good news is that at the start of 1999, CSFB had just paid out our bonuses, and we were all given a severance package. While I tried to figure out where to go next, I learned that Larry Brown, the head of Deutsche Bank's lending group, was starting a commercial mortgage-backed security lending arm. I learned of a job opening there for someone with my exact background, applied, got an offer, and took it.

A few months into working at Deutsche Bank, I got an angry call from a borrower from my CSFB days. "Rob, you got me into this loan. You've got to help me get out of it!" he screamed.

He had received a sizeable offer to buy his property and had called the servicer to ask about prepayment of his commercial loan so that he could accept the offer. The loan servicer told him that the loan couldn't be prepaid early, because that's how the contract had been written. This wasn't an oversight; it was by design.

Property mortgages are commonly bundled together and sold off as bonds, or securitized. But bonds don't do well with prepayment, so securitization lenders, such as CSFB, Freddie Mac, and others, often put a "defeasance" clause in loan agreements to prevent the loans from being prepaid. Now it had come back to bite my former client, and nobody seemed able to help him. The loan servicer he spoke to before he called me certainly had no idea how to "do a defeasance," or free up that property. "Nobody knows how to do a defeasance," the loan servicer told him. "Just forget about it."

The loan servicer was mostly correct. At the time, there were probably four or five people in the CRE world who knew what a defeasance was. The borrower simply couldn't believe this, which is why he was furious. He needed to get out of the loan and was frantically seeking a solution. As I listened to him rage over the phone, all I could think was "What do we do here?" Then, I thought of a potential business opportunity.

CREATING A DEFEASANCE PROCESS

Anyone who knew what a defeasance was said you couldn't get out of one, but I knew that wasn't true. I knew of an instance when someone "defeased" their loan. It wasn't easy. In fact, the process required several lawyers and investment banks, but that instance proved that prepayment was possible. I was determined to figure out how to do a defeasance and then make the system faster and easier.

The first defeasance I worked on was extremely expensive, but I got it done and learned a lot. With the experience I already had with lending and securities, plus the knowledge I gained doing my first defeasance, I was certain the process could be more efficient. I also knew there must be many people stuck in defeasances who wanted out, so I decided to go all in.

I left Deutsche Bank in December 1999, only months after starting there, and launched Commercial Defeasance, with the slogan "Defease with Ease." To ensure that I owned the defeasance space, I proceeded to buy every URL having to do with defeasance, as well as ads for online searches for that keyword. I put everything I had and more into that company. I sold everything I owned, got a second mortgage, and financed everything else.

In 2000, our first year in business, we did only six transactions. However, by early 2006, we were doing several thousand transactions a year. We had around 80 percent market share thanks to the hard work of essential employees like John Hosmer, Jason Kelley, Jeff Lee, and Josh Cohen.

People were making a lot of money in real estate around that time, but I started to get the sense that the bubble was going to burst. I had seen it before, back in 1991, when the RTC and FDIC came in one morning and took over seven regional banks—basically all of the banks in New Hampshire. After the takeover, the RTC foreclosed and liquidated all the banks' real estate holdings, creating a huge opportunity for real estate investors with cash. However, traditional real estate investors were shut out because they were the ones being foreclosed on. The people who had capital, such as doctors and other professional service providers who were liquid, bought valuable real estate for pennies on the dollar.

Having witnessed that, sensing we might be due for a repeat, and recognizing that being liquid was the key to being successful in a down market, I became hypersensitive to risk. So in 2006, when the private equity firm Summit Partners offered me a large sum to buy Commercial Defeasance, I followed my hunch and got out.

I was 36 years old and decided to "retire."

STARTING AGAIN AS AN ENTREPRENEUR

Retirement didn't suit me well. By 2008, I was ready to be back in business. I just needed a business to start. Once again, my family background in real estate became the key.

Ten years earlier, my dad had taught me about federal tax credits (aka section 42, the low-income housing tax credit). My dad used them to develop affordable properties throughout the country, but developers could choose to sell the tax credits for quick cash. In a good market, syndicators who bought these tax credits could then resell them at a profit. However, the buyers were then responsible for ensuring the properties remained in compliance for the 15-year tax credit period. Otherwise, the tax credits would be voided, or recaptured.

I had watched the tax credit market for years, and by 2008, it seemed to have peaked. I assumed that, in a recession, corporations wouldn't need tax credits. I expected the tax credit market was going to crash and that the syndicators, who were reselling the credits, were going to go away and that I could then step in and take over all the deals and ensure compliance. I started a company named TCAM, for Tax Credit Asset Management. Sure enough, the tax credit market dropped and some syndicators went out of business. TCAM was there with the technology and services the market needed, right when it needed them.

I hired an extremely talented leader named Jenny Netzer, who, with her team, effectively built TCAM. I provided support with strategy and marketing, but Jenny managed the day-to-day operations. The business became one of the largest independent firms in the affordable housing space.

At the same time I was growing TCAM, I started buying up properties at a deep discount, thanks to the Great Recession. The market in 2009 through 2011 had bottomed out. Over the next few years, we bought several thousand apartments, office properties, and development deals that lost their funding before they were finished.

Around 2011, my former business, Commercial Defeasance, took a nosedive, and the private equity fund who bought it from me thought if I came back, I could fix things. They sold 50 percent of the company back to me, at a steep discount compared to what I had sold it to them for just a few years earlier.

PARTNERING TO WIN

In 2013, Summit Partners and I partnered to create new businesses to support the CRE market. We developed multiple services and technology solutions, including a data and analytics company (Trader Tool), a brokerage network (QuietStream Network), a renewable energy asset manager (RadianGen), and Investor Management Services (IMS).

IMS was one of our most innovative businesses; it merged our real estate background with technology. I was able to get great information about my own real estate portfolio, but when I entered into partnerships with other owners, the information they gave me was often low quality and outdated. I wondered why there wasn't a central platform with standardized information for real estate owners and investors to see how their properties were doing and to effectively gauge performance. IMS became that solution.

IMS made the back office more efficient for owners, and featured an easy-to-use interface for both owners and investors that enabled improved communication.

Summit Partners and I ended up selling TCAM to MRI, RadianGen to Solar Plus, Trader Tool to Backshop, and IMS to RealPage. Finally, I bought the remaining portion of Commercial Defeasance.

I started Thirty Capital, a holding company for Commercial Defeasance, as well as other companies. Thirty Capital's software technology and financial advisory services portfolio includes Lobby CRE, EntityKeeper, Thirty Capital Financial, Thirty Capital Performance Group, Thirty Capital Ventures, The Academy of CRE

Finance and Innovation, and other ventures. These pioneering enterprises integrate modern technology with expert services to propel the commercial real estate industry's advancement.

My love of innovation enabled me to fuse my knowledge of CRE with capital markets and technology to create eight- and nine-figure businesses unlike any in existence. As a CRE owner, operator, and investor, I use these supporting businesses to increase the value of my portfolio, and I've seen how they increase value for my customers. In addition, decades of observation and experience have given me a sense for where the CRE industry is headed. I wrote this book to share what I know, and what I know is coming.

In this book I'll discuss how to grow your CRE business by becoming more data-driven and innovative. I'll show you how to set objectives and reach them by leveraging the data you have within your firm. The CRE best practices I share will help you support your employees and customers. You'll learn how to apply these practices to your own CRE business, whether you're just starting out, are mid-market, or are well established. And I'll share some thoughts about how to create an effective exit strategy.

I hope that, after reading this book, you come away with an enhanced understanding of the CRE market, how you can differentiate your business, and how to spot the signs and predict what the next big trend will be in order to capitalize on the opportunities.

PART 1

What Innovation Is and Why It Matters in Commercial Real Estate

WITH TENS OF THOUSANDS of CRE firms competing for properties, investors, and tenants, how can your business ever stand a chance at competing? The key is to become more data-driven and innovative.

The truth is, too few small and midmarket CRE firms are investing in strategies and tactics that will improve their businesses and the outcomes they are achieving. Many are using traditional, tried-and-true approaches that worked five decades ago but are now obsolete. If you think you can use obsolete marketing tactics and survive, much less thrive, in this market, you're very much mistaken.

Learning the basics regarding how to identify and gain a competitive advantage will enable you to recognize patterns and predict changing market dynamics before the rest of the market does. This new capability will enhance your leadership skills. Seeing beyond the building can help you leapfrog your competition.

CHAPTER 1

Driven by Data

USUALLY, THE TIME SPENT sitting in the back of the plane during a guys' ski trip is reserved for drinking, bullshitting, and playing lobster dice or other games designed to reallocate everyone's cash. But this trip in 2016 was different. While four of the guys and I—all real estate people—had been joking around en route to Jackson Hole, I realized that Mike Altman, the member of our group who was generally the loudest and most entertaining, was quietly working away on his laptop. That wasn't like Mike, who was almost always goofing off with us, so I went back to see what he was so serious about.

Mike was hard at work on an investor presentation he needed to finish up before we landed, which confused me, since pitch decks are pretty boilerplate. At least, the pitch decks I've seen usually lead with information about properties, strategy, the management team, and of course any home-run performances. Why was this taking so much of Mike's time?

Mike was the chief investment officer at Cortland, which had grown from 5,000 multifamily units to 60,000 in five years. Obviously, its strategy was working. Mike explained to me that one of Cortland's differentiators was its ability to articulate innovation. While most companies emphasized their track record, Cortland, instead, highlighted its supply chain and building materials integrations and, most importantly, its data and analytics capabilities. Cortland showed how they used those capabilities to create alpha—beating the market and generating gains above the standard market return through skill or superior strategy rather than market timing. Alpha is the benchmark that differentiates average players from exceptional ones. Mike explained that it was pure arbitrage, nothing more. No one else was doing what Cortland was doing, despite the fact that joint venture equity partners were obsessed with alpha.

It came down to being able to prove that alpha return, he told me, and Cortland's focus on innovation gave them an edge. Years before, they'd made the strategic decision to focus on and integrate innovation and data and analytics into their business. That included acquisitions, operations, finance, legal, and development—everything. Cortland made a huge investment: hiring data analysts, data scientists, and programmers, creating a team, and building its business around this team. Driven by data and what the data revealed, Cortland became a company with data and analytics at its core.

It reminded me of Wall Street as the digital revolution was taking place on the trading floor. Some traders were using Bloomberg terminals, and other, old-school traders relied on runners and phone calls to execute trades. The traders who did it the old way simply couldn't keep up. Bloomberg's innovation changed that industry. There are many other examples of industries that have embraced data and the opportunity to become innovative. Just look at hospitality and accommodations, where hotels now have to compete with home owners willing to rent out space on Airbnb, or taxis, which now have to compete with car owners willing to drive people around using Uber or Lyft, or even pizza, where Domino's is now delivering its food using driverless vehicles. Other industries are working to get ahead of the game, while commercial real estate is falling behind.

Many people in real estate still see themselves as simply owning real estate, when they should be repositioning themselves as technology companies that happen to work with real estate. That's where the future of real estate lies, and Cortland is one of the few companies that is ahead of the curve. A few years before that conversation with Mike, I had started to recognize the need to innovate in the real estate space, but I hadn't yet figured out how to put data at the center of my business operations like Mike had. Cortland is one of the largest and most successful firms in the real estate industry, and that trip with Mike helped me see how much they'd invested in innovation, changes I could make in my own businesses, and how much other firms need to catch up or risk being like the old-school stock traders after everyone began using Bloomberg terminals.

THE POWER AND POSSIBILITIES OF DATA

Once you have data—your own as well as data from outside sources—the opportunities you can spot are incredible. For example, some CRE companies track cell phones. Tracking cell phone data can tell you where people are going during the day and night, whether they are actually back to work in traditional office space, and where people are shopping, among other things. Or if you own an apartment complex and you see that your residents are traveling several miles to go to area shopping centers, is there an opportunity there? Does a closer cluster of retail stores make sense?

That's just the tip of the iceberg, really. Besides the data you can get from cell phones, such as pedestrian traffic patterns, there are an unlimited number of observations and connections you can make from data. Some obvious and not-so-obvious ones include these:

Rental property affordability

By comparing personal income with rental rates within regions or micro metropolitan statistical areas, you can see whether personal income growth is keeping pace with rental rate increases. Depending on the numbers, you may decide that it's time to sell, if personal income has flattened out. Or if rental rates are rising and expected to for several more years, maybe it's time to buy.

Residential migration patterns

Noticing where people are moving to and where they're leaving can help spotlight areas where demand is rising or where supply is expected to increase soon.

Crime statistics

Which areas are safer and which are experiencing rising crime rates? Are there shifts that might point to buying or selling opportunities?

Weather and leasing activity

Is there a correlation between when people come in to lease apartments and the weather? Based on that, you can better time your leasing hours and marketing approach.

Shipping ports

Following port traffic and observing the health of a shipping port can predict the ebb and flow of residents to an area. A rise in industrial distribution can drive demand for housing and retail in an area, just as a decline can signal it's time to get out.

These are just a few examples of CRE data points that can be closely correlated and can also be leading indicators to spot opportunities.

I started to realize the opportunities to use data in CRE in 2013. At the time, I was an active investor in lower tranche commercial mortgage-backed security bonds. These were attractive because we could underwrite the real estate risk. The challenge was that we had to underwrite a lot of properties to be able to benchmark whether an investment was good or bad. We needed thousands of properties to serve as data points, so we bought an existing due diligence and underwriting company, Fairview, and built out a data and analytics and underwriting platform, which we named Trader Tool.

It took only a few years to amass hundreds of underwriters, commercial brokers providing market feedback in several hundred markets, and thousands of commercial loans and tenants we could track. We had data. Every second of the day, data would come in and make the Trader Tool system smarter. We could identify troubled properties and value pools of mortgages.

Around that same time, I attended an industry conference. I stopped at a booth sponsored by Tableau, a leading business intelligence tool. Tableau allows the user to visualize and analyze their data, much like Excel allows you to manipulate data and generate charts. I saw incredible possibilities to import my CRE portfolio data plus commercial mortgage-backed security Trader Tool data into a business intelligence tool like Tableau.

The Tableau salesman was a master of the art of possibility. He saw he'd piqued my interest and proceeded to show me maps and charts, analytics and correlations that would synthesize all the data in my businesses. It would take all my data and give me insights I currently couldn't access. I was convinced that if I had Tableau, I'd be the smartest real estate guy in the world.

It seemed to me that all I needed to do was buy the software, attach my data, and go! I didn't consult with my IT team; I just bought Tableau on the spot.

Soon afterward, excited about the opportunity, I assembled my data team and my real estate team and pitched my idea for real estate dominance. I quickly found out I had made a big and expensive mistake. I was right about how data would change the industry, but no matter how in love I was with Tableau, it wasn't the right solution. I couldn't simply hook it up to all our data sources. It didn't speak the same language, and the work required to get our systems talking to Tableau made it impractical.

No one wants to hear that their baby is ugly or that they've bought something expensive that they didn't need, but that day, my CTO at the time, Phil Kubat, had to tell me just that. However, Phil is a professional, so he kindly said, "Let me explain data to you."

UNDERSTANDING DATA

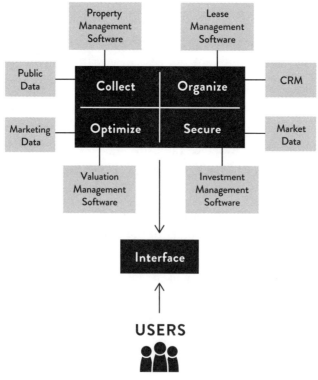

Figure 1.1

What I didn't know then but my tech team quickly explained is that a business intelligence tool is only as good as the data being entered. And every bit of data out there speaks a different language. It looks different, sounds different, and is different. To leverage data, it's critical to have a business intelligence tool and also data that's aggregated, translated, and cleaned. Having one without the other won't work. However, data management (prepping, cleaning, and sorting data) can be a big undertaking. The costs go far beyond the $50,000 business intelligence price tag, and it's an ongoing expense. My real estate companies had disparate data coming in from property management systems like Yardi or RealPage and market intelligence from Moody's or Trepp. I had dozens of data analysts working at Trader Tool to make sure the data was clean or error-free, standardized, and spoke the same language.

At Trader Tool, we sold to large institutions. They had no problem justifying Trader Tool's cost, which included not only our fees but the cost of the staff they employed to process the data. However, it was clear to me that smaller CRE firms could benefit from data as well, if they could afford it. That was a big "if," but I saw that if we could create the right system, one that worked well with standard industry data formats, and sell it on a subscription model rather than a flat fee, we could give even the smallest CRE firms access at a price point they could afford. I envisioned it working a lot like a Microsoft 365 subscription. This concept was the catalyst for Lobby CRE, a data analytics and portfolio management system we developed. Lobby CRE was the system I needed instead of Tableau, and by building the system I needed to import and analyze my data, I created an entirely new business to serve other real estate investors and operators.

I launched Lobby CRE because the philosophy that drives all of my businesses today is that data analytics should drive decisions within a company. Data doesn't lie, but data is worthless unless it helps you do your job better.

In general, people use data for four things:

- To report
- To visualize
- To analyze
- To activate or respond

Pretty basic, right? However, before a company can begin working with data, they have to collect it.

Let's face it: Most companies are already collecting data as a natural part of doing business, but it's indirect collection. They're not doing it on purpose or with any plans for what to do with it. For example, a mom-and-pop pizza shop has data available about how many pizzas they sell each night, how much pepperoni they use daily, what percentage of customers order delivery and what percentage order takeout, and many other data points. It's there for the taking, and they could access it and analyze it if they had a plan or strategy. But right now, most pizza shops—and CRE firms—have data that they're not acting on. They're not capturing or storing it for analysis and activation. Data is being generated, but it's essentially going to waste.

Every time you underwrite a deal, data is collected. Every time you shop a property, you're collecting data. Every time you get a broker's package, you're collecting data. You can count by hand how many people come in and out of a business in a day, or you can use existing data to get an accurate number, such as through counts of the door opening or by counting cash register transactions. Technology can make data gathering more accurate and more efficient. Collecting data is easy; it's what you do with that data and how you pair it with other data points that will differentiate you. That's where innovation happens.

The great thing is basic data analysis doesn't have to be complicated or expensive. It's possible to start small. You don't need pricey software or data lakes (which is really just a storage unit where your untranslated data sits until you need it) to see what's going on in your business. For many firms, Excel works just fine to organize and analyze data that has already been collected. (One caveat: You cannot scale very far with Excel.)

With the help of technology, you'll be able to collect data, analyze it, and see trends you wouldn't have recognized before. You're able to report, visualize, analyze, and activate with the help of technology tools.

EVEN BASIC DATA HELPS

One investment strategy my real estate arm frequently uses is the value-add multifamily strategy, which is fairly common. We buy or invest in apartments in good locations where there is a gap between class A and class B rents that can be reduced by upgrading the housing complex and units. One of the most basic upgrades is the appliances, but after the initial investment, they need to be maintained in order for them to hold their value.

A few years ago, we were evaluating an investment into a West Coast owner/operator who deployed this strategy. As part of the evaluation, one of the first things we do is benchmark the operating statements. Lobby CRE combines data we've gathered from broker packages with data available through our partnerships with the Institute of Real Estate Management and the National Apartment Association. The Institute of Real Estate Management data allows us to do peer-to-peer benchmarking across thousands of properties. So, when we did this, we noticed that their properties had a higher repair and maintenance number than most of the competing properties. When we explored why that was, by looking at those operating statements, we learned that this particular operator was buying appliances that cost less at acquisition but cost substantially more to operate and fix because they were not as durable. They were leaving hundreds of thousands of dollars of property value on the table by trying to save a few hundred dollars on appliances. We recognized the issue by evaluating the data. And this operator now tracks this type of data, and much more, but had to learn the hard way about its importance.

BECOMING A UNICORN

Right now, most people make decisions based on a small percentage of the data they have access to. That data may include, for example, your own experiences and those of your colleagues, combined with what you've recently read or what you learned back in school, plus internal reports someone generated. That is all data, and the result is often a gut feel or educated intuition. In many cases, that intuition is spot on. But what if it was possible to supplement that intuition with hard environmental data? The percentage of data you're using would climb from 1 percent to 5 percent or higher. And imagine what could happen if you could increase your access to data to 20 or 50 or 80 percent? The quality of your decision-making would increase tremendously!

There is a long-held belief that we use only 10 to 15 percent of our brainpower and that if we could find a way to tap into the remaining 85 to 90 percent, we would make progress so much faster. That is effectively what data and analytics enable you to do with your internal business data—to make better-informed, more effective decisions.

Research by PwC showed that data-driven organizations are three times more likely to report improvements in decision-making than organizations that are not driven by data.[1]

This is where the magic happens. As you start to change the status quo of your collection and use of the data you have around you, the potential for creativity and innovation skyrockets. The best part is that you already have plenty of data at your disposal. The first step is getting it translated so that you can tap into it and analyze it.

Leveraging their advanced quantitative training and data and analytics expertise in a new market was the goal when former Wall Street equity trader Justin Nonemaker and Eric Zagorsky, who worked in leveraged finance, turned their attention from finance to real estate. Coming out of Goldman Sachs and JP Morgan, these two pros are among the best of the best in terms of data analysis, and they recognized the opportunity to apply their expertise to an asset class where there was the opportunity for alpha.

Applying their well-honed analytical skills, Justin and Eric revealed coming opportunities in flex space and last-mile distribution and, in 2012, decided to establish Maryland-based ShoreGate Partners to pursue strategic opportunities in markets along the East Coast. They pooled investments from friends and family to get started and have never looked back. For the last 10 years, they have achieved amazing results, thanks to their data-driven approach. In fact, they've been so successful that they are closed to outside capital.

In the coming discussion, I'm going to give you the tools and the framework I've applied in our technology businesses, capital markets business, and real estate business to help you build your own data-centric organization that helps you see beyond the building too.

That is how you can increase the capability of your organization. Gather your data, analyze it, understand it, and then use it, and you'll become a data-centric, innovative company that is leaps and bounds ahead of your competition. You'll attract equity investment, you'll differentiate your firm, you'll build enterprise value, and you'll be able to spot trends and opportunities before everybody else does. But it starts with your data.

The good news is that it's doable. It's not easy, but it's possible, and it's worth it. The first step is believing that you are an innovative technology company whose product is real estate.

Next steps

To start to become a data-driven organization, your first task is to identify what your data consists of and where it resides. What you'll find is that data exists in silos, which is problematic. Next, I'll show you how to translate your data, and you'll see how innovation is all about collecting and analyzing the data you already have access to.

To get you thinking about your many data sources, table 1.1 contains a list of potential sources of data and what each can tell you.

Table 1.1. Potential sources of data.

Sources of data	Data provided
Broker packages	• Market and property comps
Construction and maintenance	• Construction costs, maintenance costs (the cost to maintain what you built)
Marketing	• Website metrics (page rank, views, key words) • Surveys • Yelp scores/google scores • Scores of surrounding properties • Traffic patterns (where do people go)
Finance	• Current loan to value and debt service coverage ratios, equity • Loan maturities • Interest only periods • Outstanding principal balance with prepayment or hedge cost • Current spread to index • Debt optimization to hold • Promote and waterfall windows • Investors' equity • Cash flow projections
Accounting	• Property financials • Balance sheets • Variance to budget • Variance to proforma • Delinquency, annual revenue
Market data	• Comps • Peer to peer benchmark • Market health (other property types)
Leasing	• Box scores • Vacancy • Lease maturities

With this list in mind, start to make your own list of potential data sources and systems. You may be astounded at the number of systems you're using.

CHAPTER 2

Leadership

WHILE MY OWN BUSINESS ventures have taught me a lot about leadership, both what to do and what not to do, some of the most valuable leadership lessons have come from leaders I've observed, known, or worked with. One of those who had a large influence on me was Willy Walker.

The first time I ever met Walker, now CEO of Walker & Dunlop, was at a National Multifamily Housing Council conference in Orlando in 2014. The conference is all about doing multifamily deals, so there are always brokers, mortgage bankers, owners, and investors all in one place, mixing and mingling. It was a sea of suits and blazers, and then I caught sight of a guy strolling through the room as if he were competing in the Tour de France. It wasn't just the brightly colored bike shirt but the skin-tight shorts, helmet, matching shoes, and bike. I'd later learn that's quintessential Willy Walker, always doing things his own way.

Doing things his own way has served Walker well in business. After taking over as CEO of the company from his father in 2007,

Walker transformed Walker & Dunlop into an agile, fast-growth venture, growing it from a privately held regional mortgage company valued at $25 million to a company with more than 1,400 employees,[1] $4.7 billion in assets,[2] and, as of March 2022, a $4.39 billion market cap.[3] It's one of the top Freddie Mac and Fannie Mae lenders.[4]

In an interview with *Connect CRE*, Walker explained that when he decided to join the business, "I didn't want to become the world's greatest mortgage banker. I was interested in building a business."[5] Innovation was the first step. As far back as 2009, the company was already an early adopter of new tech, investing heavily in databases to tap into market data and better understand how much debt and equity was outstanding across the multifamily market landscape.

During the Great Recession, Walker & Dunlop acquired companies while other firms focused on survival. These weren't just other commercial real estate companies but tech companies as well, like GeoPhy.[6] GeoPhy is an artificial intelligence and machine learning company Walker & Dunlop expects will help revolutionize the small loan and appraisal sectors.

Walker has also invested in building his personal brand. During the recession, Walker started a weekly webinar series called Walker Webcasts, and he has interviewed dozens of industry players in an effort to position himself as a leading voice of real estate finance. According to *Bisnow*, "The weekly video sessions have gone beyond business updates, tackling questions of emotional intelligence and leadership that have shown the personal side of Walker and his guests."[7]

When Walker joined the company, he set a goal to be the largest provider of capital to the multifamily industry by 2025. He achieved that goal five years early, in 2020. He did it by looking at the big picture, deciding what kind of company he wanted to run, and using innovation and technology to see where he needed to go next. He infused automation and workflow improvements into the business, as well as investing in research capabilities and data and analytics. He looked for ways to improve internal capabilities that would point to new external opportunities. Then he led his company in the direction of those opportunities, all the while fighting an uphill battle against people in his organization who were resistant to change.

Few people actually like change. It feels risky and produces anxiety, which is why so few people and companies resolve to do things differently. Not only did Walker have to win over the firm's employees, but first, he had to convince his board of directors and shareholders to trust him. He had the conviction that his strategy was going to achieve his objective of turning a regional player into a national powerhouse. The fact that he succeeded in convincing others to follow him is a true sign of his leadership abilities.

SETTING THE COURSE

While Willy Walker is not afraid of change or the challenge of innovation and reinvention, he is unusual. Not too long ago, I was talking to Sandeep Mathrani, the well-respected commercial real estate leader who took over as CEO of WeWork after its founder, Adam Neumann, was ousted. He shared with me that "the failure of companies is due to the arrogance of their leaders. They fail to reinvent and they lack fear and humility," he said. When he said they "lack fear," he meant they become complacent. Intel cofounder Andy Grove was of the same mind when he said, "Only the paranoid survive."[8] Complacency and playing it safe keeps leaders stuck on the same path, unwilling to introduce change because it may result in their downfall, rather than recognizing that failing to change and innovate guarantees the ultimate failure of the entire organization.

Leaders are the people who need to decide the purpose of the business, its goals for growth, and how that growth will occur. They're the people who have a vision of the type of organization they want to run. Their challenge is hiring good people who buy into the leader's vision and plan and then communicating that vision company-wide, so that everyone is clear about the actions they can take to achieve the firm's goals and to serve the company's purpose.

It's the leader's responsibility to lay out the plan to find a way to differentiate the business to be able to raise money for growth, to create enterprise value through investment of that money, and to spot new opportunities and trends that are worthy of investment or that are more relevant. It's also the leader's responsibility to solicit buy-in from all interested parties, from employees to customers to suppliers to boards, partners, senior management, community stakeholders, and investors.

That's exactly what Willy Walker did. He saw that the business could be more than a regional mortgage lender, so he created a plan to achieve that objective, hired smart people, let go of people who didn't buy into his vision, and got everyone aligned to drive toward their common goal. He also judiciously acquired companies that strengthened Walker & Dunlop's capabilities. That's how the firm became a multibillion-dollar enterprise in a few short years.

However, achieving organizational or cultural change is easier said than done, as organizational psychologist Jim Bright's research reports. Bright found that one in three people (34 percent) would avoid change completely if they could.[9] For those who do attempt change, they often expect immediate results. If they don't see positive results right away, 32.2 percent give up and try something else. That's what leaders like Walker are up against—a preference for the status quo on one hand and unrealistic expectations on the other.

Unifying stakeholders and persuading them to pursue a common vision for an extended period of time is what Walker did, and it's also what Alan Mulally did as CEO of Ford around the same time. Mulally left Boeing in 2006 after 37 years in various engineering and design roles to take over at Ford, which by that point was all but bankrupt.

One of Mulally's first tasks as CEO was conceiving of and sharing his new vision for the company, which was "people working together as a lean global enterprise for automotive leadership."[10] Next, he studied Ford's history to understand its current problems, resolve why they occurred, and assess what to do about them. That resulted in Mulally selling off several automotive brands, including Aston Martin, Land Rover, Jaguar, and Mazda, so that the company could focus on the Ford brand. Mulally's bigger challenge, however, was resolving long-standing interdepartmental grudges and unifying the organization. His plan was called "One Ford." He expected employees to collaborate and support each other, and he introduced new communication tools designed to infuse responsibility and accountability. The new vision and tools worked.

Ford's turnaround was dramatic and continued throughout Mulally's tenure. Ford's stock price was as low as $1.38 around the time Mulally took the helm and was $16.00 per share when he left.

He succeeded because he was able to convince the skeptics and naysayers that positive change was possible, and then he proved it. He showed them that there was a different way to operate the business and that it could be successful.

BECOMING A TECH COMPANY

Continuing to do business the way it's always been done is rarely the key to success. The key is to identify a way to differentiate the business and move in that direction. That's why the first thing leaders need to be able to do is pivot their organizations away from how they've always done business to a new approach, whether that's a new market, a new product offering, or a new marketing message.

In the case of Walker & Dunlop, Walker moved the firm away from a small, local focus and expanded into brokerage, capital markets, and advisory through its investment in technology and innovation. In doing that, Walker & Dunlop became a technology company that offers real estate services as a product. Walker made the conscious choice to pivot away from the status quo into new territory.

Other CRE firms have the same opportunity to pivot from being property owners and operators to business owners whose product is real estate. That's a key difference. It makes it possible to raise capital, to invest in the business, and to achieve growth. That's different from simply buying more buildings. I'm talking about building a corporate entity that has a competitive advantage.

THE LEADER'S ROLE

Being a business leader is different from being a CRE pro. The skills required to run a business involve making investments in infrastructure, establishing business processes, and hiring talented people.

I started Commercial Defeasance when I was 29, and the average age of my employees was probably mid-20s, many having joined right out of school. Because of the youth and relative lack of experience of my team, as well as my own immaturity, I was more like a college football coach than a true leader. I was part teacher, part cheerleader, and part dictator. I had to take raw talent and ambition and teach my team members how to be successful, often step-by-step. To achieve progress, I frequently felt I had to demand performance of my team, to strong-arm them into doing what I wanted them to do.

As I've matured and the composition of my team has changed, I'm now more like an NFL coach, and my employees are more like Tom Brady. Rather than demanding performance, I provide a goal and some guidance on how to get there, and if the employees can't or won't do what they need to do, then I find someone who will. I don't have to provide basic training in how to do their jobs. I let the professionals on my team do what they're capable of, and if they're not capable, that becomes apparent and we part ways. I don't badger, micromanage, threaten, or yell at them the way a college football coach and some CEOs might try to motivate a team member.

The role of a leader, of a CEO, today is so different and much more difficult than even a few years ago. On top of internal pressures to perform and grow, CEOs have external and social pressures that are becoming bigger factors, and they need to be addressed. Today, a CEO is more often held responsible for the happiness and well-being of their employees.

Being a leader isn't just about the business decisions to be made but also about how work gets done by the people who are responsible for that work. And if you can't straddle the line between managing people and helping them enjoy their work, as is now required during the Great Resignation, attracting and retaining quality employees will continue to be a challenge. Many people today can make more money staying home than they can working for you; just look at the rise in side hustles and small businesses since 2020. For many, the choice not to work for someone else's company is an easy one. That's what you're up against as a leader today.

It's much easier to galvanize people and get them all moving the company in the same direction when the leader can demonstrate a track record of success. My company, Thirty Capital, was just voted the best workplace in Charlotte, North Carolina. That kind of recognition motivates our team to do even better work, and creates a culture that attracts A players and weeds out those who aren't the right fit.

KNOW YOUR STRENGTHS

Leaders who are self-aware can leverage their strengths while also taking steps to rectify or correct their weaknesses. Understanding your strengths and weaknesses as a leader—and we all have leadership capabilities to some degree—makes it much easier to be effective. More effective leaders are able to initiate change and achieve organizational objectives faster. And speed is important, especially when exploring or pursuing new business opportunities. The faster you can research and investigate potential opportunities, the better your company's chances of obtaining first mover advantage in the marketplace.

So, what is the process for determining your strengths and weaknesses? There are tools designed to tell you where you are strong and where you are weak. There are assessments you can complete or online tests that will give you an objective look at your own personal advantages and disadvantages and how you can use them to be more successful.

A few years ago, I took the CliftonStrengths assessment to understand my own strengths and weaknesses. The results were helpful and confirmed some suspicions I'd had about my personality. It also helped me understand how I come across to others. According to CliftonStrengths, my top five strengths are futuristic, adaptability, maximizer, ideation, and activator. Apparently, that means that I'm very future oriented. The assessment indicates that I can recognize patterns or signals that help me anticipate what I need or my business needs to be successful.

The assessment also confirmed that communication was not one of my strengths. It's number 13, although I really expected it to be even lower than that. That means that although the vision is clear in my head, I have difficulty expressing it to the people around me. It's really frustrating for them and for me. I also discovered that I needed help in organizing my thoughts and ideas. Analysis as a strength was number 28, which means it's more like a weakness. Because my thoughts aren't as organized as other people's, when I share them, the information doesn't flow in a logical manner.

However, once I started addressing my communication weaknesses and learning how to better articulate my vision, everyone benefited. We could all level up our performance. The company's success began to steadily increase. But it all started with me evaluating, then addressing, then building on my own strengths and weaknesses. All leaders should stop and consider their own strengths and weaknesses and how best to leverage them or mitigate the damage.

For example, after learning that my communication skills might be even worse than I previously realized, I now ask people on my team to repeat back to me what they think they've heard when I talk to them. After I share information in, say, a product meeting, I'll ask the person I was talking to, "Could you repeat back to me what I just said?" This isn't a test or meant to put them on the spot about their listening skills. Rather, it's a step I can take to confirm that the person I'm speaking to understood what I was trying to convey. If they can't parrot back to me what I've said, then I need to try again by restating my point a different way. This is the extra step I've built into my operations in an effort to ensure that I'm communicating clearly, now that I know it's a major weakness of mine.

Everyone has different strengths and weaknesses, but it's not possible to work on vulnerabilities unless they've been identified.

SETTING THE COURSE FOR SUCCESS

The CEO needs to steer the ship. They have to set the vision, share the vision, and map out the plan to achieve the vision. So if, as CEO, your vision is to become the largest owner/operator of multifamily housing, you need to make sure everyone in your company understands that's the organization's ultimate goal. Then you can explain the strategies you'll use to realize that vision. Or if you want to become the largest distributor of capital, then that vision will take you down a different path. It's the leader's job to get everyone on the same page.

To do that, to rally the troops, requires a three-part process:

Vision

Your vision is your high-level description of what you want your company to do, be, or have. It's your 50,000-foot set of goals. How is your business positioned in the marketplace? What is its reputation? What are its competitive advantages? Paint a picture for others that articulates where you want your company to be in the (not-so-distant) future.

Voice

The next step is communicating to your employees how this vision will be achieved. It's making sure everyone understands and believes in the direction the company is headed.

Direction

And the direction involves determining what steps are involved in pursuing this vision. It's the "how." What do you need in order to successfully execute?

Next steps

Leaders have many different attributes, but knowing your strengths and weaknesses can give anyone a leg up in performing at their best. To identify and assess which of your personality traits and skills are advantages and which may be disadvantages, consider taking an online assessment. Some of the most popular today are listed below:

- CliftonStrengths
- DiSC
- HIGH5
- Relational Needs
- RoundPegg

PART 2

Modern Best Practices in Commercial Real Estate

ONCE YOU UNDERSTAND HOW critical acquiring a competitive advantage is and you recognize that such an advantage is possible by leveraging the data within your organization, it is time to apply the best practices in your planning and with your employees and customers. The innovation framework, which you'll read about here, is key.

In particular, learning about OKRs and KPIs is a core lesson here, to assist in setting and tracking the results that will fuel future growth and success. Applying what you learn from this section will enable you to level up your business and spot future business opportunities and potential threats before they can negatively impact your company.

CHAPTER 3

Planning

ONLY AT A 50,000-FOOT vantage point, where you can see your entire CRE enterprise as a whole, can you see what's beyond the building. That's where you notice big opportunities. That's where you create alpha. That's where you create differentiation. And that's where effective planning starts.

That's different from the bottom-up approach that many CRE firms take. The traditional approach starts with a foundation, literal and figurative, and works up from there, building at each step. That means starting with properties and then figuring out what needs to be done to each property to ready them for lease, whether that's doing electrical or plumbing work, for example, then marketing, showing, leasing, and maintaining, at least in the case of multifamily housing. The focus is on readying each property to be rented so it can generate revenue. Then the revenue from each property is aggregated to determine what the company can earn in a year. That's the standard approach, and it's getting in the way of your success.

In CRE, we plan on many fronts. We plan annual budgets, capex budgets, marketing plans, resident–tenant engagement plans, refinance plans—even landscaping plans. But do we plan for our business of running real estate? No, not the way we should. Most CRE firms continue to operate as product-based businesses, rather than as the technology companies they need to become. Too many CRE firms are focused on individual properties when planning, instead of viewing the whole enterprise, including the complete property portfolio, as the business. It's the difference between taking a 5,000-foot and a 50,000-foot view.

COMMERCIAL REAL ESTATE FIRMS AS TECHNOLOGY VENTURES

By thinking of CRE firms as technology companies, it makes sense to look to the darlings of the tech world to inform how these firms should be planning. Almost all of the tech industry success stories have the same thing in common: the use of the OKR framework. OKR stands for *objectives and key results* and was a management practice developed at Oracle but popularized and adopted by Google, which uses them company-wide to keep everyone focused on outcomes.

The OKR framework has been adopted across the technology space for several reasons. One is that OKRs define the why, the how, and the what for the firm at every level, which is critical for getting alignment. But more importantly, OKRs link activities, which create outputs, with the desired results. Outcomes drive impact. And by clarifying the outcome you're working to achieve, you can create a virtuous cycle of purpose and motivation company-wide. In other words, OKRs make sure everyone is doing what they are supposed to be doing.

As indicated by its name, there are two components of OKRs: the objectives and the key results. Objectives are the big-picture vision. They are broad and ambitious, setting the long-term direction for the company for the next three to five years. Key results are derived from those objectives and are specific, measurable, time based, and actionable. They are a lot like the next level down in an outline, in that they make up the OKRs. They help define what success looks like on the way to achieving the larger company objective.

It's imperative that firms write down objectives, their corporate goals, and share them with the rest of the company; a lack of alignment across all employee levels will slow progress. To achieve company goals efficiently, everyone, including the CEO, the vice president, the manager, the property manager, and the janitorial staff, needs to be aligned with the company's objectives and must understand how their individual work can impact it. Everyone also needs to understand who is responsible for what, and why a particular outcome is critically important to the business.

When I started Lobby CRE, my goal for the business was to be the premier data and analytics platform for CRE owners. To accomplish that, we established plans and milestones for the business and then cascaded them throughout the organization, from senior leadership to our functional teams, and then to individuals.

At the organization level, we had three defined objectives: growth, people development, and execution excellence. Then within each objective, we had two key metrics: Within growth, we had recurring revenue growth rate and net user retention. Within people development, we had the internal promotion ratio and employee satisfaction. And within execution excellence, we had the client referral ratio and the operating margin. That was it. Simple, right?

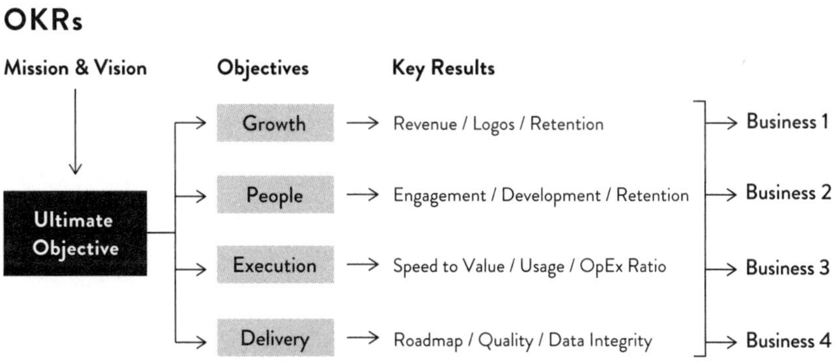

OKRs

Figure 3.1

We kept our OKRs simple for a reason: We wanted them to be able to fit on a business card. That way, every employee could quickly refer to them anytime a question came up about the appropriate decision or direction. On one side of the business card was the organizational OKRs, so that everyone would be united in working toward our common goal, and, on the other, was each team's specific OKRs, so that every team member understood how they could contribute to the company's success.

We intentionally created a balance between our metrics, too. For example, it's great to increase revenue but not at the expense of retention. Or it's great to increase revenue but not without maintaining our operating margin.

After testing OKRs within Lobby CRE, we replicated a similar process within our CRE business. OKRs provided an opportunity for increased clarity within the organization, which we discovered we desperately needed at our Amarillo property.

Five or six years ago, we wanted to reduce vacancies at that property—which was one of our growth-related objectives—so we created incentives for our property manager there to increase occupancy. She went to work, and in no time, occupancy was at over 90 percent. We were impressed at how fast she worked. Part of her sense of urgency probably had to do with the bonus structure we set up for her. Because she immediately addressed the issue of lower-than-desired occupancy, she quickly made money hand over fist.

Unfortunately, we set up the reward system the wrong way. Her process for filling vacant units was not aligned with the actual result we wanted to see. She heard "fill vacant units" above all else and ended up ignoring the qualifications of some of our prospective tenants. What we really wanted was sustainable increases in revenue to boost net operating income, not merely full units. Because of our mistake, we filled units with tenants who couldn't really afford to live there, which led to delinquencies, bad debt, and evictions.

Once we clarified the organization's objectives and communicated them to the property manager, she felt empowered to better manage the property, without micromanagement from the regional manager, the asset manager, and the firm owners. The objectives, results, and impacts were clearly aligned, and as she worked in this new system, she could easily show decisions and actions she took to achieve the results and the impact the company wanted. From then on, she filled the units with qualified tenants who stayed long term.

BEST-IN-CLASS COMPANIES

Using OKRs, we set broad objectives and expectations for our organizational strategy across the company's whole property portfolio. But that still provided the flexibility and specificity for regional and property managers to pursue those results however they saw fit. They still had ownership of those key results.

Planning is all about what you want to be as the owner of CRE, as the owner of a company. You may have different business units within your company, but together they form the organization. I often explain the ideal company structure using Mondelēz, which is the company that owns Nabisco, as an example. Nabisco is a food company made up of many divisions, all of which are snack products—cookies and crackers, mainly. Within its cracker business unit, for example, they have Wheat Thins and Triscuit and Cheese Nips and Chicken in a Biskit. In order to grow the Mondelēz organization as a whole, the company plans where it wants to be in terms of revenue and profits within each brand, within each business unit, *and* within the corporation as a whole, rather than focusing specifically on growing, say, the salty snacks division.[1]

Mondelēz thinks in terms of owning the snack food segment and what it can do to get Mondelēz snacks into every home's pantry in the US, for example. That's the outcome they're pursuing, using the output of a larger share of that total market. In recent years, efforts to do that have involved beefing up its ecommerce presence as a whole, which proved instrumental during the pandemic, as customers began buying online at much higher rates.[2] The expansion of its ecommerce channels, which provided a way to fatten margins by going direct to consumer and eliminating the costly middleman, was another output aimed at achieving the larger objective of growing the business. Sales in 2020 at Mondelēz were up, hitting $26.6 billion.[3] By 2022, they were at $28.6 billion.[4]

Another company that was extremely successful because of its focus on the larger picture was ITT, which was run by famed manager Harold Geneen. I know a lot about Harold Geneen because my father made me read his book, *Managing*, early in my career.[5] Although the book is slightly outdated at this point, I would recommend it to anyone in business. It certainly shaped how I think about gathering and analyzing data, business growth, and management.

Harold's claim to fame was having taken ITT from a troubled telecommunications firm to "a colossus with more than 375,000 employees and $16.7 billion in revenue," according to his *New York Times* obituary.[6] Along with rising sales, earnings per share grew an average of 10 percent per year for 58 consecutive quarters.

At the heart of Harold's success was his understanding that "for a true multinational conglomerate to operate efficiently, control was everything."[7] Not surprisingly, Harold was compared to dictatorial leaders like General Patton, Alexander the Great, and Napoleon.

Despite this tough approach, Harold did a lot of things right in business. For one, he bought up companies to add to the value of his conglomerate. ITT, at one point, owned 350 companies in 80 countries and was in industries ranging from food service to car rental, construction, grass seeds, outdoor advertising, insurance, and hotels. ITT was diverse in a way few other corporations were.[8]

At the heart of his organizational strategy was "to give his managers overlapping responsibilities so that checks and balances existed on everyone."[9] Harold also needed to know everything about everyone and everything that had to do with his company. He required managers to prepare detailed weekly and monthly reports, to keep him informed about their parts of the companies. He wanted data, and lots of it, in order to make better decisions about the company's operations. Updates on KPIs and metrics were critical elements of his process.[10]

He also held monthly meetings for 100+ ITT executives, which lasted a week and ran from 10:00 a.m. to 10:00 p.m. daily. During those 12-hour days, those in attendance would work through problems that had come up and develop policies to reduce future issues in all divisions. The attendees were Harold's de facto advisory board, helping to contextualize the data that they were evaluating and to decide the best course of action for the parent organization.

To prepare for those meetings, every one of the 250+ division leaders wrote a report that went straight to Harold, and these reports were used to set the monthly agenda. One of his rules was "no surprises," and thanks to these lengthy reports, there rarely were any.

Surprises are rare when expectations are clear, when systems are in place for communication, and when there is alignment across the company, where everyone can tie every action or initiative to a larger goal that supports the company. Whatever that ultimate corporate goal is informs annual company goals, which then determine team OKRs and metrics, which then set individual contributor actions and daily activities.

That's why, after committing to the OKR framework at Lobby CRE, we automated OKR reporting to distribute information up, down, and across the whole organization for visibility and to hold our people accountable for knowing their numbers. That's why we don't need monthly 12-hour meetings to recalibrate and check in (and who has the time, really?). With easy access to OKRs and metrics, we can quickly pinpoint where we need to focus. We address concerns before they become problems or impact our outcome, share best practices quickly, and are able to see and celebrate successes.

THE PLANNING PROCESS

The type of planning needed within a company depends on whether it is strategic, which looks three to five years out; tactical, which is for quarterly and monthly objectives; or operational, which is for weekly or daily tasks.

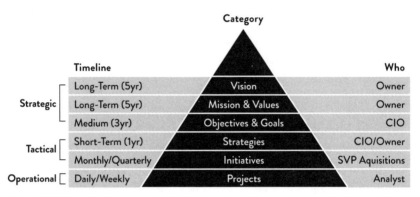

Figure 3.2. Your planning pyramid should first start with your company's vision and its mission and values.

Step 1: Vision and mission statements

The first step in planning with OKRs is to establish your firm's ultimate objective, which is your vision coupled with your mission and values for it. This statement establishes *why* your company exists and *how* it creates and delivers value for the world.

In defining your vision, which is the 5- to 10-year outcome you want to achieve within the business, consider the following questions to guide you to one simple statement that encompasses that vision.

- Where do we want to go?
- What can we realistically achieve?
- What problem do we intend to solve?
- What are the changes we believe we can make for the world?

- How will things be different if the vision is realized?
- What phrases or keywords describe the type of outcome we want?

Those considerations should then lead you to that one statement that represents the company's vision for the future. For example, it might be "to provide the premier neighborhood experience to working families." What is it you want the company to do, be, or have? Why does it exist? That's the vision.

Then, your mission defines the company's purpose in the world, in one simple statement. This is the *how* piece, the one statement that reflects how you'll achieve your vision. In the previous CRE example, your mission might then explain the goal of "serving as a positive force in the community."

Then you put the two statements together to form your ultimate objective: "Providing the premier neighborhood experience to working families in order to serve as a positive force in the community."

Take Tesla's vision, for example. It wants "to accelerate the world's transition to sustainable energy."[11] That is the company's "why." Its mission is "to create the most compelling car company of the 21st century, while accelerating the world's transition to electric vehicles."[12] Its mission takes the vision a step further in terms of specificity. It wants to accelerate the world's transition to sustainable energy by driving that transition to electric vehicles.

Swedish home furnishings company IKEA's vision is "to create a better everyday life for the many people."[13] Its mission is to "offer a wide range of well-designed, functional home furnishing products at prices so low that as many people as possible will be able to afford them."[14] Together, its ultimate objective is "to create a better everyday life for people by offering a range of well-designed, functional home products at prices so low that as many people as possible will be able to afford them."

Or there is Amazon's vision, which is "to be Earth's most customer-centric company, where customers can find and discover anything they might want to buy online."[15] Its mission is this: "We strive to offer our customers the lowest possible prices, the best available selection, and the utmost convenience."[16] Together, those two statements create the company's ultimate objective, which is "to be Earth's most customer-centric company by offering our customers the lowest prices, best available selection, and utmost convenience."

Your vision and mission statements, together, should paint a picture of where your company is heading. That's the long-term ideal, though, and the next step is bringing that overarching goal down into more actionable objectives at the company level.

Step 2: Objectives

In the OKR framework, after establishing your company's vision and mission, it's time to establish your organizational objectives. To do that, you take your ultimate objective—that big-picture, 10-year view of the world—and break it down into shorter-term objectives. These are more 3- to 5-year objectives, rather than 10.

When drafting these organizational objectives, you'll want to follow some OKR guidelines:

- Objectives are broad, directional, and visionary in nature.
- Objectives do not include numbers, metrics, or KPIs.
- Objectives do not dictate specific actions, projects, or initiatives.

Think in terms of themes. What are the most impactful layers of your business that you have authority over and that will create the outcomes defined in your ultimate objective? Are these levers possible sources of market or competitive differentiation?

Once you have a good list, share them with your leadership team for opinions, comments, suggestions, and feedback. Not only does this provide input regarding how to better tailor those organizational objectives, but it also serves to get buy-in from your leadership team and helps ensure that each leader and their teams are included both in the process and the work toward these objectives. You should end with no more than three objectives total.

At this next level of planning—tactical—senior managers must translate top-level goals and objectives into quarterly and monthly strategies and initiatives. They need to break those larger goals down and delegate tasks to reach them. For example, a goal of adding 12 new properties to the company's property portfolio next year means that an average of one new property a month needs to be bought. Identifying what kind of activities and staffing levels are needed to support that top-line goal is what managers deal with at this level.

By breaking large goals down into bite-size pieces, they can easily be delegated and acted on. In addition, by insisting that all activities, no matter how small, can be traced back to a larger goal, leadership can ensure time is not wasted on irrelevant tasks.

Step 3: Key results

After establishing your organizational objectives, the next step is creating organizational key results. A key result defines what success looks like when the objective is achieved.

Each of your three objectives from step 2 should have one to three unique key results associated with it. As you're establishing key results, keep the following guidelines in mind:

- Key results can be defined in one of two ways: showing progress, not perfection, through significant progress toward a result or reaching a minimum viable threshold—meaning the result is at least as good as the defined minimum.

- Key results are specific, measurable, and time bound. What's the metric you're going to track to demonstrate success in obtaining the result and outcome you were after?
- Key results are ambitious, achievable, and actionable. They should be challenging to reach, but not impossible; your key results should also be tied to initiatives, projects, and jobs to be done.
- Key results are designed to hit metric-driven milestones, which are then celebrated and recalibrated to set a new higher or better threshold.
- Key results do not involve dictating projects or initiatives for your team but, rather, the outcome you want to achieve.

To develop key results, brainstorm as many as you can and then share with your leadership team for input and constructive criticism. Don't be surprised if you get pushback or debate here. You're done when you have no more than three key results for each objective.

Step 4: Initiatives and projects
Getting ever more detailed, the next step is to define the initiatives and projects that your company will need to undertake in order to accomplish each objective and set of key results. I call this the "What do we need to do to drive these key results and achieve the objectives?" stage.

Step 5: Review, clarify, simplify
To finalize the objectives and key results at the senior leadership level, the last step is to review them, then clarify and simplify where needed.

Once you have completed the five steps for the entire organization, it's time to move to the next level down in the organization.

Once the organizational initiatives are established, each senior leader works through the same steps with their direct reports, to align each of their objectives, key results, and initiatives to the OKRs above. Each level checks against the level above. For example, the senior leaders will review with the C-suite before cascading down to their direct reports and teams.

As you move through each level of the company, it's important to get buy-in. Forcing initiatives and projects onto your teams won't yield the results you're after. Sharing data and being transparent about progress to OKRs is also essential. It's critical to accountability.

Be aware that having everything go smoothly the first time you work through the process is unlikely. It's okay to update OKRs when it makes sense to do so, such as after achieving a key result. But if you do decide to make a change to an OKR, be sure your reasoning is clear, rational, and easily understood by everyone in the company. It's better to overcommunicate the change in direction and start fresh with the process than to stay focused on OKRs that don't make sense for the company anymore, whatever the reason.

INCORPORATING DATA INTO YOUR PLANNING PROCESS

The planning process for any organization starts with looking at historical figures (if you have them): Where has the company been, and where is it headed? Then based on that data, the business can set top-line growth goals. Are you hoping to increase the number of properties you own, to improve tenant retention, to change your brand's image? What's your big-picture goal?

Most CRE owners know where they want to be in the coming months and years, although they may not always share those figures. But they should. In order to get the whole organization rallying behind the firm's performance targets, employees first need to know what those targets are, and their compensation should be aligned to the organization's purpose, mission, and values.

If you're trying to build a brand, instead of reaching revenue targets, you're more likely to be monitoring metrics such as Glassdoor ratings, which reflect what it's like to work for the business, or net promoter scores to understand how satisfied customers are and how willing they are to recommend the company to others.

The next step is breaking down company-wide performance targets into increasingly detailed goals and figures.

Table 3.1 shows what the math looks like when you break down a goal of owning 5,000 units in five years, taking into account assumptions based on past performance.

Breaking down this big goal into ever-smaller goals makes it achievable, makes it actionable, and you're empowering your talent to do the job they were hired to do. You start with a big-picture goal, such as owning 5,000 units in five years, and you identify all the building blocks it will take in order to achieve that goal. You'll need outside investment, and properties, and hiring, but exactly how much of each depends on the data.

IT ALL COMES BACK TO DATA

To break down the larger, company-level goal, you need data. How many deals do you need to underwrite to hit your portfolio target? How many deals do you need to do? How many people do you need on staff to do those deals?

In the technology world, we talk in terms of annual recurring revenue. So, we might say, "In four years, we need to have $10 million of annual recurring revenue." There's also monthly recurring revenue.

Then, when we draft our business plans and budgets and go to raise equity funding or take on debt, it's all based on hitting these goals we've set. In many cases, it becomes a math problem: If I need

Table 3.1. Market rate multifamily

Assumptions					
Average number of units	250				
Average performance unit price	$100,000.00				
Average deal size	$25,000,000				
Regional equity average	$7,500,000				
Acquisitions analyst use	**Conversion**	**Day**	**Week**	**Month**	**Year**
Number of deals initial Scrub	100.00%	4	20	80	960
Number of deals to underwrite	50.00%	2	10	40	480
Number of deals to incentive compensation	33.00%	0.66	3.3	13.2	158.4
Number of deals to letter of intent	66.00%	0.4356	2.178	8.712	104.544
Number of deals to best and final	2.00%	0.008712	0.04356	0.17424	2.09088
Number of deals to close	50.00%	0.004356	0.02178	0.08712	1.04544
Goal	**1,000**	**Units**			
Number of deals initial Scrub	3,840				
Number of deals to underwrite	1,920				
Number of deals to incentive compensation	634				
Number of deals to letter of intent	418				
Number of deals to best and final	8				
Number of deals to close	4				

to have $10 million of annual recurring revenue and my average sales price is $100,000, then I know I need to do 100 deals in the next three to five years. That's a fairly easy number to get.

Once we know we need to do 100 deals, then we can calculate how many deals we need per week, what kind of turnover we should expect, how many properties we need to underwrite per week, and how many properties then need to be analyzed in order to underwrite that number. Each new data point helps us break down that goal into actionable steps we need to take, or initiatives to reach, as far as purchases and deals go.

CREATING ENTERPRISE VALUE

This bottom-up approach can hamper your ability to create enterprise value because it puts a lot of control and power in the hands of people who may not have the big picture of what you're trying to achieve. Unless you consistently share the company's goals and strategies for reaching them, employees will be unlikely to understand the role they need to play. They need to understand how their job and tasks are aligned with the overall objective. Otherwise, you will encounter issues that interfere with hitting your KPIs. You need to communicate with all employees regularly to keep everyone aligned and working toward the same objectives.

Next steps

With the proper tools and processes in place, you make plans, execute them, analyze, and adjust. Download my OKR template at https://robfinlay.com/books/beyond-the-building to run numbers for your firm and develop your own OKRs.

CHAPTER 4

Key Performance Indicators

OKRS ARE YOUR HIGH-LEVEL targets or desired results. Once you've set those objectives, it's important to then track them using key performance indicators, or KPIs. The KPIs are your scorecard.

OKRs and KPIs work in concert with one another. OKRs define the strategic direction of the organization with a key result being the desired outcome. KPIs are the indicators—how you measure those key results to determine whether you're pointed in that direction. KPIs also help maintain the baseline performance necessary to keep the business running. Put another way, there are two ways to use KPIs: as leading indicators for your key results and as steady-state performance metrics to assess the overall health of the business.

Successful CRE firms pay attention both to what's going well in the business and what's not. That way, they can do more of what works and less of what doesn't. Knowing where your time and resources will yield the biggest impact or are most needed is critical business information. That's where OKRs and KPIs come into play. Firms in virtually every industry, from CRE to finance, manufacturing, service, online—you name it—use KPIs to gauge how the business is performing and identify where their focus should be targeted.

I want you to build a business around excellence—excellence in operating, owning, managing, and investing in real estate. I'm assuming you already know how to measure the performance of an individual property using metrics like occupancy, net operating income, and its growth. Most firms do that. However, too few firms analyze KPIs for the company *as a whole* and instead focus on minutiae related to individual properties.

Property KPIs that many firms already use fall into four categories, all having to do with deal pipeline:

- Leasing
- Financial debt and equity
- Market
- Investor

These are all specific to individual properties. For example, worrying about leasing issues like concessions in one building or vacancy rates in another are property-level problems. Although you certainly want to address those problems, they are unlikely to make or break the entire company. Focusing too hard on smaller factors can prevent your company from growing. Although that statement may make sense conceptually, it can be challenging to apply. So, let's use a different business as an analogy to explore company-level KPIs.

Let's talk about plumbers, because plumbers require training and skill in order to build a solid business. If you were looking to acquire a plumbing business, would you assess how the plumber unclogs a toilet or the brand of PVC pipe they use? Is that going to tell you whether the business is doing well?

No. In fact, I'd argue that those types of details have little to do with how the *business* is performing. Sure, if you're considering hiring an individual plumber to work in one of your properties, you'd want to evaluate their skills at handling common tasks like stopping water leaks and replacing piping, but if you're trying to value the business—the plumbing company—you need to analyze very different metrics.

You'd want to examine the attributes of the business that make it successful. Those would likely include how quickly employees respond to customer calls, how satisfied the plumbing customers are, how much of their business comes from referrals or repeat customers, how well their advertising performs, and how efficient the staff is with their time. What makes the business profitable, which is the foundation of its current success, is how the company is run. And that requires more than just knowing how to deal with a burst pipe.

KPIs in a CRE firm need to deal more with branding, the cost of customer acquisition, net promoter scores, and operational metrics having to do with vacancy and rental rates at the individual property level. KPIs are better at the property level if they are consistent across the company's portfolio.

OKRS AND KPIS IN AN URBAN VILLAGE

One of the best examples of companies that successfully create and implement OKRs and KPIs throughout the organization is OpenPath Investments. OpenPath is a very successful midmarket multifamily investor. When its founder, Peter Slaugh, realized that his residents were looking for a sense of community and that his investors wanted to make more impactful investments, he developed the concept of the urban village to address both customers' needs. The urban village is about embracing and fostering engagement in residential communities, which then helps improve tenant retention and, ultimately, profitability and a number of other important metrics.

Within OKRs, we track certain key performance indicators as leading indicators, or early signs of outcomes, and others as lagging indicators, or outcomes of achieving results, that are cascaded to the property level to track the tactical things they do as a community.

For example, here are several potential urban village OKRs and their respective KPIs.[1]

Table 4.1. Urban village OKRs and respective KPIs

OKR	Key Result	KPI
Building community	Resident engagement ratio	• Diversity and inclusion (leading indicator, ensures our team reflects the diversity of our residents) • Event hosting ratio (leading indicator, resident-led versus OpenPath-led, to ensure residents and volunteers are empowered to drive engagement in the community) • Median participation frequency (leading indicator, ensures it's not the same core group of participants) • Resident satisfaction score (lagging indicator, ensures that residents are satisfied with their community) • Resident retention (lagging indicator, ensures that unit turnover doesn't adversely affect financial performance)
Channeling resources	Reduced cost of living expenses	• Active partnerships (leading indicator, ensures residents are connected to social and economic resources) • Partnership adoption (leading indicator, ensures residents are using partnerships) • Percent delinquency shielded (lagging indicator, ensures residents are able to pay their rent without unexpected delinquency) • Resident rent-to-income ratio (lagging indicator, ensures compliance with policies or regulations)
Developing leaders	Community leader ratio	• Resident rent concession (lagging indicator, ensures that rent concessions deliver value back to the community) • Leader retention (lagging indicator, ensures that OpenPath captures the value of the investment in training) • Training hours per month (leading indicator, ensures a pipeline of leaders and active facilitators) • Resident leader to UV talent conversion (leading indicator, ensures healthy pipeline for UV open roles) • Employee net promoter score (can be both leading and lagging, since if your organization's score improves, it means improved results will probably follow, and if your organization's score is higher than those of competing firms, you will likely outperform the market. However, it can be a lagging indicator as well, in that after implementing improvements in your business, it takes time for the score to improve.)
Enhancing environment	Percent CapEx environmental improvements	• Number of environmental improvements/property (leading indicator) • Utility usage/property (lagging indicator) • Carbon emissions/property (lagging indicator) • Financial investment-to-return ratio (lagging indicator) • Rebates and incentives earned (lagging indicator)

But what about other roles and operations that aren't covered directly by OKRs, like maintenance requests, marketing and leasing performance, and others? Although these may impact the OKRs, the relationship to them is indirect.

To address these, OpenPath uses KPIs to measure the health and foundation of the business, in addition to the KPIs above to assess the impact of the OKRs.

THE KPIS YOU SHOULD BE PAYING ATTENTION TO

Although there are likely thousands of possible data points you could track, there's a point at which it becomes unrealistic to monitor every possible metric that could impact your company. Unless a particular factor has a significant impact on your business, tracking it may not be worth your time. It's up to you to determine what makes sense for your business.

However, on a corporate level, there are many data points *everyone* should be using. These are the base numbers on your standard chart of accounts and include the following:

- Deals in the door
- Deals underwritten
- Deals quoted
- Bids
- Deals under contract
- Deals closed
- Investor satisfaction
- Investor churn
- Repeat investors
- Investor touchpoints per deal

- Satisfaction scores
- Glassdoor reviews
- Employee churn
- Employee length of stay
- Net promoter score
- Tenant satisfaction
- Apartment ratings

This is not a complete list. You'll want to create KPIs that correspond to your own OKRs.

Looking at company-wide data points like these is what will help you attract outside institutional capital in order to create enterprise value and spot opportunities and trends in the market. Your success lies in monitoring your KPIs.

KPI ROLE MODEL

The real pioneer of KPIs in CRE was the late Byron Cocke, who was way ahead of his time. Byron was all about KPIs and metrics and constantly preached about the importance of using technology to monitor KPIs, to better manage businesses. His obsession with numbers and commitment to religiously monitoring KPIs allowed him and his partner to grow their Atlanta-based real estate and investment management firm Cocke Finkelstein, Inc., into a property investment management venture.

Byron was all in on using data and technology because he saw it as a source of innovation. He understood that data and analytics were tools for doing things differently. If you adopt the same obsession with numbers, data, technology, and innovation, you'll be on the path to fantastic growth within your business.

PLANNING FOR GROWTH

To use KPIs, it's important to start with high-level goals for your business—your OKRs. These are the big-picture objectives. What is it you want your business to achieve within the next 36 months? Setting these goals will then help you derive the KPIs to support those goals.

For example, if your goal is to increase acquisitions in the coming year, your first step is to set a top-line goal. How many properties do you plan on acquiring? Are you shooting for 5 or 50, for example?

Next, you'll want to look at your previous internal data to determine the data points surrounding your historical acquisitions, but especially in the last year. What does your data tell you in terms of how many properties your firm is capable of finding, evaluating, making an offer on, and acquiring? Knowing how many properties you acquired in the previous year is a starting point, supported by other KPIs, to help you set parallel goals. That is, if you want to acquire 10 new properties in the next 12 months, you should go back and see how many properties you had to analyze before you could make an offer on 1. Then see how many offers led to purchases.

If you know that it takes, on average, 10 properties to get to 1 offer and 1 in 4 offers results in a purchase, you can do the math to find out you have to evaluate 40 properties for each potential acquisition. And if your goal is to acquire 10 properties, that means you'll need to plan on analyzing 400 (10 × 40).

Knowing that number, you can evaluate your resources to determine whether that goal is realistic. Can you actually identify and process 400 properties in a year? If not, what's a more reasonable goal?

Your KPIs inform those goals. They allow you to identify, diagnose, solve, and verify that solution. A KPI success story will illustrate how valuable they are.

Joe Lubeck is the CEO of American Landmark, one of the fastest growing multifamily owner/operators in the US. Based in

Tampa, Florida, American Landmark owns and operates more than 32,000 multifamily units in communities in Florida, Georgia, North Carolina, South Carolina, Tennessee, and Texas.[2] The company's success is due in part to Lubeck's insistence on the use of KPIs across all aspects of the business. The company's mission has always been to deliver great service and outstanding living environments to tenants; attractive, risk-adjusted returns to investors and partners; and opportunities for growth and advancement to its diverse team members.[3]

American Landmark has reaped the benefits by monitoring and tracking a core set of KPIs. In 2021, Lubeck rolled out Landmark 360 to track a series of KPIs around resident engagement, resident behavior, and resident satisfaction.[4] By monitoring these KPIs closely, the company was able to create initiatives that not only benefit their other properties but also increase resident metrics.

By looking at the KPIs from a portfolio perspective, rather than examining individual properties, Lubeck is better able to make data-driven decisions that serve all three of his company's constituents: tenants, investors, and employees.[5]

At the core of Landmark 360 is regular data gathering from tenants through surveys, to understand what they want and need from their housing. On top of tracking resident engagement, satisfaction, and behavior, American Landmark also monitors investor engagement, satisfaction, and behavior, as well as employee engagement, satisfaction, and behavior.[6]

Through KPI tracking at a corporate level, Lubeck and his team have recognized the interconnected, almost symbiotic relationship between tenants, investors, and employees. That is, employee satisfaction impacts resident engagement, which impacts investor satisfaction, just as tenant behavior impacts employee satisfaction and investor engagement.[7]

Monitoring and tracking KPIs informs important business decisions that affect all of the company's constituents.

KPIS LEAVE CLUES

In addition to aiding in goal setting, you can look back over your KPIs for clues as to why you're having problems in various parts of your business; these may suggest where you are weak. For example, if you see your portfolio's Yelp score is a three out of five, that may hint at some work you need to do to improve the ratings tenants are giving your properties. Why aren't they all fives?

You should be able to look back at your baseline to see which properties are underperforming so you can address issues there—specifically to get that larger, portfolio-level Yelp score up. For example, if most properties are rated between 4.5 and 4.9 but one is rated a 2, it's clear where your attention needs to be focused to bring that average portfolio-level score up.

BENCHMARKING

Regular reporting of KPIs provides a continuous feedback loop so you can spot numbers that diverge from your average or target score. Starting with a baseline number for each KPI allows you to spot improvement or decline.

KPIs are also important because they define the health of the organization, which can determine your company's valuation. Technology companies—as yours now is—like software as a service (SaaS) companies, are valued on a handful of metrics. KPIs allow companies in the same industry to be compared across several factors and include numbers such as customer lifetime value, customer acquisition cost, and compound annual growth rate.

These standard metrics are what industry insiders and investors use to compare various players, to see which companies are strong performers and which ones are weak and in what aspects of their businesses. These KPIs are typically more important than the company's core product. Most software companies don't make a profit, but as long as your KPIs are above average, you're doing okay, many investors would say.

It all comes back to alpha, as I mentioned earlier. Alpha is the excess return over and above the benchmark for the industry or market. Your goal is to create alpha, across all properties, so that the company as a whole earns alpha. The only way to do that is by attracting and retaining high-performance employees, knowing your customer, and planning for growth.

Doing as well as everyone else doesn't create alpha. Only by being better, by exceeding the benchmark across multiple KPIs, can you hope to generate alpha. Setting and then religiously monitoring your company-wide KPIs will give you the best chance for success in CRE.

Next steps

Each company has its own KPIs that leadership has decided are the most important numbers to track. No two companies will be the same; however, there are some standard KPIs that SaaS companies use that you should consider at least as a starting point. You can download these KPIs here: https://robfinlay.com/books/beyond-the-building.

CHAPTER 5

Employees

YOUR PEOPLE ARE ONE of your biggest assets, if not *the* biggest asset. Yes, data is important, but people are even more so. We're witnessing an increase in demand for both talent and data skills. That's why the hiring of data analysts within CRE firms is on an upswing, and more than one in three CRE companies is refreshing talent and recruitment strategies to shift to future technology and skills needs.[1] As the industry rushes to embrace data, between 2017 and 2021, the proportion of CRE organizations that expect to be "data-driven" doubled to 56 percent.[2]

Blackstone, for example, has invested heavily in people and tools to better manage its $411 billion portfolio of commercial and residential properties. Its proprietary tool—developed in-house—named REDD for Real Estate Data Direct, is designed to collect, store, analyze, and report data to both employees and investors.

Blackstone's recent hiring patterns are evidence of a company that has recognized it needs skilled people to access and understand the data within the organization. In recent months, Blackstone has advertised multiple openings for analysts, data analysts, data engineers, financial data analysts, and data scientists, among others. It has also created a functional group called Blackstone Data Science, which is "a team of data scientists, strategists, and engineers that uses data to . . . [analyze] complex datasets, [develop] predictive and analytical models, and [help] the firm use data more effectively."[3]

Blackstone illustrates the need for data professionals to make sense of all the data your company has access to. Data is important, but it's worthless without employees or consultants who can collect, analyze, interpret, and share it with key stakeholders. You need the right people on your team to execute your plans and goals. You can have all the data and analytical tools to process it, but unless you have the right people in the right roles in your company, you won't be successful.

It's time to embrace the industry's increasing reliance on data by adding talent. Ignore it at your peril. Firms that decide to put off investing in people trained to manage and study their data will be vulnerable to competitors that do. They are the companies that will be the next Blockbuster or Kmart.

To avoid that fate, start by looking at who you have on your team right now.

YOUR CURRENT ORGANIZATION CHART

If you look at the standard organization chart at most CRE firms, you'll see there is an individual or a team responsible for buying properties, someone responsible for operating them, and someone who deals with the finances. Typically, the names on those responsibilities are acquisitions, operations, and finance, although in some firms you might also see construction or development. These three roles are must-haves in CRE, although in smaller firms you may only have one or two people who are responsible for all three of the activities. The structure probably looks something like this:

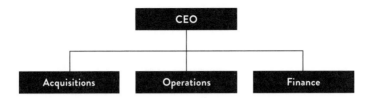

Figure 5.1. Many CRE firms have three basic functions, shown here. All employees fall into one of these three functional areas or departments.

So even if you're running a CRE partnership with a small team, you could have one partner who is an extrovert with a huge network of industry contacts and who is in charge of deals; they're the acquisitions department. The other partner, who is more of a numbers guru, handles the finance and operations side of the business.

WHAT YOUR ORGANIZATION CHART SHOULD LOOK LIKE

I want to recommend a new version of a CRE firm's organization chart, which has two additional functional roles that you need to define immediately (if you haven't already). That doesn't mean that you necessarily have to hire more employees, however; only that you need to assign these responsibilities to people on your staff—existing or new. You may already have team members who are more than capable of assuming these new responsibilities in addition to the ones they have, or you may decide to increase your head count; that's up to you. The key is that whomever you give these job functions to must own that responsibility.

The first role to add is that of data analyst, and the second is a director of engagement.

Once these roles are implemented, either with existing staff or new hires, your new organization chart will look like that shown in figure 5.2.

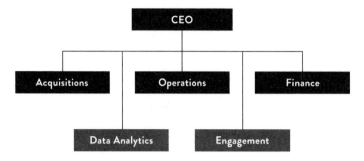

Figure 5.2. What your org chart should look like.

You'll see that two new functional departments have been introduced to manage the data and analytics side and the customer engagement activities. There could be one person in each role or multiple people, depending on your current organizational structure and needs.

You likely have people in your organization who have been handling these data analyst and engagement responsibilities as part of their official job, and just as likely those tasks have been spread out over several people, rather than sitting with one. Given how spread out these responsibilities have naturally been, you likely haven't been making good use of all the data that is available to you. Going forward, these new roles need to be at the core of your organization.

THE DATA ANALYST

No matter what size your company, you have piles of data: from your underwriting analyst cranking through deals, from your finance group analyzing financials and performance, and from your operations group evaluating income statements. You're surrounded by data, even though you may not have realized it. However, your company's ability to analyze and profit from that data may vary, as shown in figure 5.3. What are your company's capabilities when it comes to data?

My org can put data from different sources or systems into one place.

My org can access data from one common place reliably and consistently.

My org can visualize KPI trends by refreshing data.

My org can act alongside the data and insights to see the outcomes of those actions.

My org can centralize data to one trusted common place.

My org can define KPIs to monitor and report on.

My org expects data-driven insights from every member of the team to influence decisions and action.

My org can spot macro and micro trends, model those trends, and predict their outcome.

Figure 5.3

As your data collection systems become more advanced, your organization has to follow suit. It must bring in advanced capabilities to take advantage of all the usable data it has access to. As your capabilities increase, your company will move on the organizational continuum from having basic analysts to having data analysts and then sometimes data scientists at the far end of the spectrum. However, not every firm is going to reach a point at which they need data scientists (in fact, most won't). You don't need a data scientist unless you want to look for deep patterns in your data, and you have enough data for a data scientist to analyze and dig through. Even if you don't need a data scientist, it's important to know what a data scientist does. A data scientist takes data in its structured form and runs mathematical calculations and analyses on the data. This can be very useful when you're dealing with hundreds of thousands of records. However, most CRE firms don't have anywhere near that, which makes hiring a data scientist overkill. It reminds me of a Capital One ad featuring basketball legend Charles Barkley being picked first for a game of children's basketball.[4]

Every CRE leader needs to make data and analytics a core component of their business. The more data you have, use, and analyze, the more powerful your organization will become. It can be intoxicating!

Fortunately, you don't have to make the shift to become data-centric overnight. It can be done gradually. Or there are companies that can provide you with data management solutions.

No matter what you decide, the key is to combine your data with a business intelligence tool to tap into the power of the data within your organization.

Now that you see the importance of having data analysts or staff with data analysis skills on your team, there are more questions to answer, such as what exact skills are needed, do you have someone with those skills on your team already or someone who can be trained in those skills, or will you have to go outside your organization to hire someone?

Many CRE firms already have people with data analysis capabilities. You can identify them because they're pros with Excel. Most college graduates who took a finance or business class have at least some familiarity with how Excel works and can often become excellent data analysts with the right training.

Whether externally or internally, we often find candidates are strong in either data or real estate, but not both. If a new hire has a background in data, we teach them real estate, and if their background is real estate, we teach them data. (You can find a detailed job description for the data analysts we hire in the appendix.) Ultimately, a data analyst needs to understand the business, how data increases the value of the business, and how the duties they perform help us become data-centric. The duties of the data analyst include bringing data in, making sure it's correct, organizing it, putting it into storage, and finally, being able to use that data for visualization, reporting, analysis, or activation.

In addition to any customized training you might do for your CRE data analysts (we actually created an academy to train our staff), I suggest using one of the following education platforms:

- TheAcademyofCRE.com
- Lynda.com
- Udemy.com
- Coursera.org
- edX.org

The types of classes you should look for may include these:

- Data analysis
- Data cleaning
- Data collection
- Data visualization

It's important that you steer clear of super technical programming classes, however, such as Python and NumPy. These can be overwhelming and unnecessary. I would go as far as training an analyst on SQL at the beginning and leave anything more advanced for later.

Once trained, your CRE data analyst will examine data and rely on tools such as business intelligence to interpret it. Before anyone can interpret data, the first step is to translate it. Once your data is translated and structured, the second step is to buy a business intelligence tool for your analysts to use to understand your data and what it's telling you. A potential third step is to consider buying a data management platform. You can buy one off the shelf or you can build it yourself, if you or someone on your team is technically proficient.

Between hiring and training staff, buying technology tools, and incorporating data processes into all aspects of your business, you're going to expend significant time, effort, and money. I won't minimize the investment you'll need to make, but it is well worth it.

THE DIRECTOR OF ENGAGEMENT

The second essential role you need to add to your organization is that of director of engagement. This engagement role within your organization is critical but isn't difficult to hire for. Anyone with a background in marketing, customer experience, customer engagement, or even customer procurement may qualify for this role. One essential skill your director of engagement must possess is the ability to understand customers and customer journeys. A customer journey refers to an individual and the path they take on the way to becoming a customer. The customer journey may start when a potential customer sees an advertisement or hears about your company from a friend or social media post. This may lead to them viewing your website or contacting your company. The customer journey reaches fruition when the prospective customer becomes a true customer.

The director of engagement is the strategist responsible for creating customer or buyer personas—descriptions of your target customers that go beyond simple demographics to include details about their lifestyle, daily activities, needs and desires, and how they make decisions. The director of engagement works to develop and understand personas for all the types of customers your organization may have. They then monitor your customers' actions and gather feedback. Books like *Building a StoryBrand* by Donald Miller and free classes and videos at HubSpot or SurveyMonkey have been helpful in my companies to help us increase engagement and monitor the feedback we receive.

The director of engagement enrolls internal constituents within the organization, such as employees and partners, and together they develop "wants and fears boards," a tool to help understand any uncertainty and tension, internal or external, that constituents may feel about any particular initiative. The director also creates KPIs to gauge the effectiveness of these strategies. They maintain a continuous loop of engagement as they gather feedback and adjust strategies based on KPIs.

In addition to their work internally, the director of engagement works with external constituents, including tenants, vendors, and investors. To provide a simple example of what the director of engagement might do, let's say that I decide my target customer is family offices. The director of engagement will develop a strategy to connect with the decision-makers at family offices. They'll research and create different personas for those offices, they'll create wants and fears boards, and they'll use this information to create marketing materials to acquire and engage those customers.

Once the process is in place, it comes down to repeating and fine-tuning that feedback loop. In a nutshell, you first decide who your customers are; next, segment them into personas; and then break down their wants, needs, and fears to help you design marketing materials that speak directly to those issues. Finally, you track your results to see what works, and do more of what is effective and less of what isn't. It's a continuous feedback loop that improves over time as you gather more information.

ADDING TALENT

Ensuring that the core roles of CRE data analyst and director of engagement are filled within your organization is critical for your transition to a data-centric organization. However, don't get scared; filling these roles shouldn't be difficult. As stated above, there's a decent chance someone within your organization is already doing part or all of these tasks. If not, training someone internally isn't too difficult, or even hiring from outside shouldn't be too much of a struggle. Adding these two core roles will be key to making the transition into a technology company.

A perfect example of a company that successfully implemented these roles is Sterling Properties. Sterling is a multifaceted development organization with a wide range of upscale multifamily real estate holdings throughout New York, New Jersey, Pennsylvania, and Connecticut. Sterling consistently invests in its employees, providing education and opportunities for advancement that have resulted in strong corporate performance and extremely low turnover. While every business owner says the same thing about their own company, in Sterling's case, its employees are truly the firm's competitive advantage. The folks at Sterling are masters at helping each employee maximize their potential, resulting in impressive results for the company as a whole.

Steven Katz and his brother-in-law Wayne Zuckerman founded Sterling in 1993. They recognized early on that hiring analytical people and great marketers and placing them in the right jobs would be the key to the company's success. This became a core part of their focus.

They initially slotted new hires into roles based on the company's existing needs, although everyone knew the role they started with might not be where they ended up. There was plenty of shifting and adjusting as Sterling Properties discovered what an employee's skills and aptitude were.

Katz and Zuckerman worked hard to find where each employee fit best within the company, and provided the training required to help them succeed in their current and future roles. This approach allowed their employees to evolve with the business, moving from entry-level jobs into mid- and upper-level management positions.

For example, in its earliest days, the firm hired a high school student to work as a receptionist. They observed that she was capable of handling a wide range of tasks beyond purely administrative functions, so after graduation, they hired her full time, and through the years she worked in many roles. The firm constantly assessed her skills and supported her growth, and she now runs the lion's share of Sterling Properties' apartments.

The key for Sterling Properties has been welcoming its employees as members of the family. In return for hard work and loyalty, Katz and Zuckerman promote from within as often as possible. They work hard to challenge their staff as much as they want to be challenged and to advance them as they want to be advanced. In return, the company is breaking records left and right.

Determining the best way for your organization to enhance its skill sets in analytics, engagement, or other areas is critical for employee growth and retention, as well as for business success. Although data and technology are potential sources of competitive advantage, they are useless without skilled employees. You need skilled talent that can grow with the business in order to see what's coming.

Next steps

The people currently on your staff may or may not have the skills you need to grow a data-driven organization. It's time to assess your current talent, your future needs, and where you can improve in terms of specific skills. You'll find the blank matrix below at https://robfinlay.com/books/beyond-the-building, where you can fill in details regarding your company. Missing skills can be added through new hires or more training of existing employees.

Current position or job requirements	Current employees with skills	Skills required of new employees
Analyst	Use Excel, do VLOOKUPs	Use data management system

CHAPTER 6

Who Is Your Customer?

WANT TO TAKE YOUR organization to the next level? Then you need to know who your customers are. I would even go so far as to argue that your customer value equals your enterprise value. That is, the way your customers—all of them—feel about you is the true value of your company. If they think highly of you, your company value will rise, because you'll have investors who want to give you money, employees who want to work for you, and residents or tenants who will pay to be in your properties long term. Your customers help create your brand, which is the key to enterprise value. It all comes down to knowing your customers.

Armed with a deep understanding of who your customers are, what they want and value, where they can be found, and why they do business with you, there's no stopping your business growth. Giving your customers exactly what they want and in alignment with what you can provide will increase their loyalty to you and attract more customers like them. That's the essence of personalization. Just look at how specifically ads are served up on social media, based on the posts you like, the ads you look at, and the Google searches you conduct. Social media advertisers quickly learn what users are interested in, and they serve up what they're looking for. You can do the same—deliver exactly what your customer wants, when they want it. That's how your company will create and increase enterprise value.

Your company's success starts with your customers. To attract customers, you need to position your firm as a desirable partner, employer, or investor. Many CRE firms think of tenants as their customers or their investors—people who are paying money to occupy space within their properties or invest in them. That's too limiting a definition for our purposes.

Your customers are your stakeholders, the people who have some kind of business relationship with your firm. That includes investors, brokers, lenders, employees, contractors, and tenants. To be successful, you must attract and engage with each of these customer segments.

Identifying who your customers currently are is the first step in drilling down to really understand what they want and need and how you can best serve them. Then you can lead your market by anticipating customer needs and preferences. Once you know your customers inside and out, you can market to and engage them, capturing a larger share of their business and making more money.

CREATING CUSTOMER CATEGORIES

To start studying your business, make a list of all the different types of business relationships you have; these are your customer categories. I sometimes call them "customer buckets," because each grouping has different wants and needs. For example, employees have very different wants and needs from your business than, say, lenders or contractors. So, think through all of the different types of customers you currently serve.

Some may buy from you, such as tenants. Some may earn money from you, such as employees and hired contractors. Some may supply funding to do more deals, such as lenders and investors. There are other categories I haven't listed, such as government agencies or community groups, that may apply to your CRE business. Table 6.1 shows how you can associate different customer categories with company goals as well as what you can provide to each category.

Table 6.1. Customer categories and company goals

Customer	Company goals	What you can provide
Investor	Greater investment, referrals	Better returns on their investment
Employees	Lower turnover, better net promoter score	Salary and wages, supportive work environment, benefits
Brokers	More deal flow, off-market deals	More deals, higher value deals, certainty of close
Tenants	Brand loyalty	Better space, enhanced amenities, excellent customer service

Once you have identified your customer categories, it's time to break them each down into customer personas, or more detailed descriptions of the traits of those categories. You may also have heard them called "archetypes."

DEVELOPING CUSTOMER PERSONAS

Your customer categories are general, high-level labels for different stakeholder groups. But when we get more granular, we can spot similarities within each group that differentiates them from the other customer categories. Ultimately, we can get more and more detailed until we develop a customer persona, a fictional representation of a customer that sounds as though we're talking about a real person. Personas are useful for your business because they help you see your firm from your customer's perspective. This will help you determine how best to position your firm for growth in each of those categories.

IDENTIFY ROLES WITHIN CATEGORIES

To continue developing customer personas, we go one level down in granularity below your basic categories. Within the employee category, for example, you could consider executives, managers, and professionals. For the investor category, you might have large institutions, family offices, and small retail investors. Lenders might include banks, private lenders, or securitized lenders.

Define individual details

In the next step on the way to developing customer personas, describe individuals in terms of the typical person you would expect to deal with. For example, let's say your research shows that the manager of a family office is very often a male in his 50s who is conservative and likes to play golf. Maybe your typical professional employee is an ambitious woman in her 30s with an advanced degree.

As you think about a typical representative for each of your customer personas, think about how you would describe them. I'm not talking about discriminating against certain types of customers or finding ways not to serve them, but about trying to understand who your best customers are, based on demographics and other details. Basic demographics may include:

- Age
- Gender

- Income level
- Race
- Employment
- Location
- Homeownership
- Level of education

This isn't an exhaustive list, and you will likely think of other traits that stand out in connection with a customer category that you can add here. As you think of each type of customer, try and make a mental picture of them. Write down what you see in your mind's eye.

WHAT ARE YOUR CUSTOMERS' WANTS AND NEEDS?

After demographics, the next element in constructing your personas is to shift to psychographics, or the attitudes and concerns of your customers. What is it that they value? What are their priorities? And what keeps them up at night? That is, what are their wants, needs, and fears? Understanding your customers' psychographics is even more important than demographics, because it gets to the heart of how they think and make decisions. Knowing what your customers want and what they want to avoid can help you in your marketing and other dealings with them.

Here are some examples. Let's say in your experience, you've seen that the family office manager commonly values transparency, good reporting, and decent returns. He's a reasonable guy, but he fears loss of capital most of all. His nightmare is another Bernie Madoff scenario that causes losses. He's more afraid of loss of capital than loss of profit, which means your marketing message to a family office manager needs to present the opportunity differently than if you were speaking to a retail investor, who is more concerned with profit and appreciation.

Your tenants, on the other hand, could care less about capital, profits, or appreciation—they care about safety, convenience, and cost. Perhaps through customer surveys you discover that safety is their biggest concern. That impacts how you communicate with them and the words you use in your marketing message to attract and keep them.

If you know that contractors are generally strapped for cash, you may want to differentiate your firm by ensuring they get paid in 10 days, to help ease their business cash flow. Or if you know that many of your employees are in the stage of life where they're buying homes, you could make home-buying support or a signing bonus part of your offer of employment. If they're typically young parents, maybe you'd want to consider setting up an on-site day care or providing a child care subsidy.

I can't stress this enough: Recognizing your customers' needs and wants and fears makes it possible to develop detailed personas that will help you craft effective marketing messages. Once engaged, you will be able to give them exactly what they want, help them avoid what they fear, and continue serving them for the long term. You will develop trust with all those you serve, and you will be able to build long-term value in your company. The more you are seen as a preferred CRE firm, the easier it becomes to secure investment capital, find good deals, hire skilled contractors, and attract talented employees—and keep them! Success breeds success, and it starts with understanding who your best customers are and what's important to them.

Developing personas will help your firm speak directly to each type of customer. Since many CRE firms take a one-size-fits-all approach to their market, you can help your firm stand out by developing custom messaging and demonstrating that you've put real effort into understanding your customers and their situation. In turn, the understanding you gain from developing personas will help your firm to create innovative solutions to better service their individual needs. Michael Episcope's experience as cofounder of Origin Investments, a leading real estate investment company, is a great example of this in action.

Back around 2015, Origin focused exclusively on delivering high-quality real estate investments to retail investors. Michael saw how the customer experience for individual investors was different from that for institutional real estate investors—meaning it was terrible. Individuals were generally investing in lower-quality opportunities with inexperienced sponsors who charged high fees, while institutions were able to secure high-quality sponsors and negotiate fair fee structures because of their ability to write large checks. Every facet of the individual's experience was less than that of their larger counterpart. When it came to reporting, there was no transparency or any way to easily track property performance or manage their portfolios.

Michael understood his customer well and recognized how much they would benefit from an investor management portal, so Origin built it. This was an expensive proposition with no real way to measure the benefits, but it was consistent with the company's mission of transforming the way individuals invest in real estate. Providing great customer experience and transparency to the Origin investor base created a sense of loyalty, and referrals grew immensely over the next 12 months. Origin was the pioneer in creating a Charles Schwab–like experience for retail investing, where every piece of information about the investors' real estate portfolio was visible in one place. Origin was ahead of the curve.

Origin believes in innovation, they invest in innovation, and they continually lead innovative solutions, but they are innovation leaders only because they understand what their customers need and want. By building personas, you can gain a deep understanding of your customers' needs and wants to build an innovation culture like Michael did at Origin.

USING YOUR PERSONAS TO CREATE A BRAND MESSAGE

The exercise you just went through of identifying your stakeholders, breaking down each category of customer into more specific types, and then assessing them to determine what you want to attract and developing customer personas was done to improve your marketing efforts. When you're clear about who your target customers are and what they want and need from you, you can craft a marketing message and materials that speak directly to them and clearly demonstrate you're the best fit for their needs.

Many CRE firms do a great job of marketing their individual properties. They're clear about the brand image they want to present to the marketplace and the type of tenant they want to attract, and they create a set of amenities to appeal to that customer. In many ways, that marketing process is similar to marketing a hotel property. And the companies that match their marketing message to the target tenant are successful—meaning very profitable.

However, building a business, a company, is not just crafting a marketing message for an individual property in a portfolio. Many smaller companies try to build a brand property by property, rather than by the company at large, whereas larger firms have already recognized the value of branding.

I'm talking about creating a marketing message and corresponding brand image for the CRE firm as a whole. The difference is that you likely have multiple properties under management, and they're likely each different in some way. But altogether, there must be something that you can use as a common thread to brand your firm. Maybe the common thread is convenience, because you ensure that your properties are near all the amenities tenants want and need. Maybe the thread is luxury, because your team and company operations present an upscale appearance. Maybe it's technology, if your business relies heavily on it and your properties feature the latest tech tools.

One example is Brady Sullivan, a New England–based CRE firm. The company is an active developer and operator of multifamily properties in New Hampshire, Massachusetts, and Rhode Island that then links them together with a common name, which, in this case, is "The Lofts." The company owns and manages The Lofts at Mill West, Lofts 34, and The Lofts at Jefferson Mill, to name a few. Now when prospective tenants in New England are looking for loft living, they're likely to think of Brady Sullivan because the firm has claimed that Lofts brand as its own.

So, what is it that makes your company a standout? What's your competitive advantage? Is it your locations, the amenities your properties feature, the price point you specialize in, the types of customers you serve, or something else? That should be your starting point. Now you just need to confirm that the advantage you possess addresses your target customers' wants and needs. If it doesn't, find something else, because if your customer doesn't care about the advantage you're leveraging, it's not an advantage *to them.*

First, however, you'll want to work through the previous steps, starting with identifying the different types of stakeholders, or customers, you serve, followed by breaking those larger categories into smaller ones as you get clearer about your target customers—the ones you want more of. Then, when you have your various customer types laid out, you can get more specific about those customers' characteristics and what they're looking for and expecting from you; that's developing customer personas. Understanding what your customer wants can only make your marketing message more effective. Understanding your customer enables you to talk directly to your customer's needs, wants, fears, and aspirations.

When you're clear about who your individual customer is and what they want from you, think about where they turn for information. Find out what your customer watches, listens to, or is interested in, and then get in front of them.

For example, if your lender customer base reads *The Wall Street Journal* religiously, you should invest in being seen there, either through advertising or publicity. Or if your employee customer is likely to have attended a university like MIT, then invest in attracting eyeballs through an event for MIT alums, by purchasing ads in university publications or working through their career services office. If you know your target tenants are hockey fans, sponsoring a third-tier team could be well worth the money. If you're finding that your online newsletter isn't getting read, consider pivoting to a print newsletter. The Association of National Advertisers studied the ROI for electronic and print newsletters across several industries and found email newsletters had an ROI of 93 percent, whereas printed versions, despite costing more, generated an ROI of 112 percent.[1] Email is quick, easy, and inexpensive, but isn't necessarily opened. Our firm owns senior housing, and we've found that with those customers, handwritten cards get opened much more frequently than emails.

Your options are nearly limitless, really, but don't get overwhelmed. Limit your marketing efforts to those that will get you in front of your customers, wherever they are. That's the best use of your marketing dollars.

Next steps

Now it's time for you to work through your own marketing breakdown. We use storyboards, which are just a set of boxes that capture each step in this process. They look something like what you see in figure 6.1:

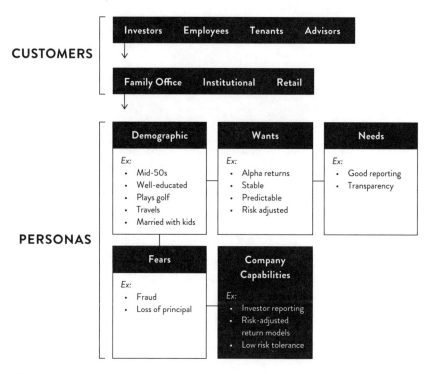

Figure 6.1

PART 3

Customizing Best Practices to Your Firm

NOT ALL CRE FIRMS are created equal. The size and maturity of your company will determine both the "what" and "how" of the actions you take, so I've divided firms by size, and offer specific recommendations for emerging, midmarket, and corporate or institutional CRE firms. Although the number of properties owned defines whether a firm is an emerging venture, midmarket, or larger CRE player, there is no judgment in those terms. I only use them to differentiate between the complexity (meaning the number of people) of the organizational infrastructure.

The next steps are all about applying the innovation framework to your business, based on your firm's current size and maturity, and what your business priorities are. Depending on where you are on the growth curve, your priority may be finding new deals or investors (probably both), or it may be building the organizational infrastructure.

Some of you are happy where you are, but there is always a benefit to applying the framework. These three areas are, to varying degrees, where CRE firms should be dedicating their resources.

CHAPTER 7

Emerging Firms

EMERGING FIRMS, IN PARTICULAR, may be more likely to be seeking out deals or finding investors, although building out their organization should also be on their radar. I would say that the resources allocated to these three parts are probably not equal. How these priorities are broken down depends entirely on where the firm is in its growth. For example, if the firm has investors, then the focus should be on finding deals and developing the organization. If the firm has deals but no investors, then the focus shifts. And if it has deals and money but isn't managing the operations well, then the bulk of the focus should be on developing internal operations.

My point is, generally speaking, most real estate companies should allocate their time and resources among three things—differentiating the firm, creating enterprise value, and spotting trends—then, tactically use these principles to find deals and investors, and to create world-class organizations.

Forward-thinking CRE firms today are looking for ways to use data and analytics to improve and grow the business and be innovative. Many owners and partners understand that to future-proof the business, they need to act more like a technology company.

If you are a one-person operation with one property, the way you leverage the available data and innovate in your organization will be different from how a multibillion-dollar venture with hundreds of properties does. Larger ventures have more resources, but they also have more bureaucracy that can significantly slow progress.

When I speak to emerging groups about the innovation framework, my audience usually consists of company principals. Within emerging firms like yours, most of what I suggest are things you have to do yourself, because you don't have a massive staff to delegate to. For that reason, you need to prioritize what you want to accomplish.

THE ADVANTAGE OF BEING SMALLER

The good news is that it's much easier for a smaller, more nimble player to become a technology company than it is for a mega corporation. You have a clean slate. You aren't bogged down by legacy systems, bureaucracy, or established processes. Without people who resist change, companies can grow much faster.

Take Max Bresner, for example. Max was the COO of BLDG Management and BMC Investments, a midsize multifamily investor, developer, and manager, before going out on his own to start Brikwell, another real estate investment firm, with partners Jake Gannon and Tyler Elick. While at BMC, Max was consumed by finding new opportunities and was a key driver behind the massive growth those two companies achieved. Because they were growing so quickly (from 25 employees and 650 apartments in 2013 to 250 employees and 8,000 apartments in 2020), however, establishing an internal infrastructure just wasn't possible.[1] The team couldn't stop midstream to begin to build internal systems without losing momentum. They didn't have the time or enough resources.

But now that Max is running his own business, he is hyperfo-cused on establishing a backbone with internal processes and systems on which to build. As part of his job, he spends an equal amount of time seeking out deals and investors as he does figuring out effi-ciencies and establishing the internal operating systems the business needs. Max knows that in order to effectively scale, he needs to make the most of every minute and use software and technology to be inno-vative and to differentiate Brikwell from other firms. For example, Brikwell is using foreign labor and software to cost effectively track and funnel its pipeline of new opportunities.[2]

Although Max clearly isn't afraid of change, he is unusual in that respect. Most people want to stick with the tried-and-true ways of doing things. According to Deloitte, 60 to 70 percent of large-scale efforts to introduce change within organizations fail because of the natural human tendency to want to avoid it.[3] And the more employ-ees work against change, improvement, or innovation, the greater the odds such efforts won't succeed.

There is always someone who wants to push back against change. Even if they recognize that such change is progress or will improve operations, they want to keep doing things the way they've always done them, because it's familiar to them. They are the people who tell others, "Here's how we do it" because, to them, there is only one way, and it's the old way. That unwillingness to learn and change and grow will impede innovation within the organization, unfortunately. And the larger the company, the larger the impact of such resistance to change.[4]

Therein lies the opportunity for smaller and midsize companies. Because it's easier to get the entire team rallying around internal changes and improvements when you're running a 5-person or 50-person operation rather than a 5,000-person company, smaller firms can make headway faster in becoming data-centric organizations.

Companies that are willing to continue doing things the way they've always been done will stagnate. There will be no innovation because it's effectively been outlawed.

THE INNOVATION FRAMEWORK

The key to success as an emerging firm is to develop a plan of attack for becoming a more innovative venture. That entails demonstrating leadership commitment, which can be shared through mission and vision statements, followed by a plan; then, evaluating your current organization and roles, as well as future roles needed to become innovative and data-centric; and finally, determining how best to use your economic resources to initiate change.

So, where do you start?

LEADERSHIP

Because you've picked up this book to learn about innovation, change, and data and analytics, you've taken that important first step: being a leader. By making innovation the mantra of your organization, you are setting it up for success. You've already read that as the leader of your emerging CRE firm, you need to first decide what kind of company you want to run. What kind of business do you want to lead? What does it look like? How large is it? What types of properties do you own?

Once you're clear on what you want your firm to look like, you are ready to use innovation and technology to determine which business opportunities are going to move the company in that direction. That could involve using automation and workflow improvements, investing in research capabilities and data and analytics, or introducing tools to improve internal capabilities.

You need to reverse engineer your vision for your company—describing the vision you have for the business and then determining what steps and resources will get you there. Then it's all about implementation, guided by your leadership. You get to make the decisions about what is done, how, and when.

Use the data you currently have to paint the picture of where you want your company to go and the additional data you'll need to map its course.

OKRS AND GOALS

In addition to the information I shared about OKRs and goals earlier, at this stage of entrepreneurial development in your firm, I ask you to set four additional OKRs to answer these points:

- How your brand will set your business apart; what do you do that is different from the thousands of others that do the same?
- How you'll buy your assets and what the key result is
- How you'll secure investors and what the key result is
- What operational excellence looks like in your firm and what the key result is

Next, you need to create the KPIs that tie into those four OKRs. That is, for each OKR, what are the two or three KPIs required to hit each objective?

You don't have to make this complex or super involved. Excel works just fine for setting up your OKRs and KPIs and then regularly tracking your progress on each metric; you don't need to invest in an expensive, high-powered system at this stage. My point is this: The principle is more important than the way you actually track your data.

EMPLOYEES

Emerging businesses can't always afford to immediately bring on a full staff. For many, increasing your head count needs to be a careful, gradual process. But you still need to add some new responsibilities, and whether you spread them out across your current staff or add new employees or contractors to take on the work is up to you.

If you don't have the resources or the need to hire right now, the two main activities you'll need to assign to current team members are data and analytics and engagement. You need people focused on those in order to grow the business.

As I've mentioned before, as an emerging venture, you don't need a full-time data analytics team to start, nor do you need a data warehouse or a full-time engagement manager. You need to reallocate some of the time your team spends at work to data and analytics, but it can be one small part of their official job, rather than a separate full-time equivalent role.

Even without additional staff, you can set KPIs, create plans, and initiate new marketing strategies. The decision then becomes whether you, as the managing partner, are taking those activities onto your plate or whether you're able to delegate them to other team members.

And if you were already planning to add some more employees, first conduct a SWOT (strengths, weaknesses, opportunities, and threats) analysis to better understand the capabilities and expertise you have on your team and where your organization is weak. Then hire to fill the gaps. If you're not sure who to hire first, I always recommend hiring an analytical person, because you can leverage their skills across multiple roles if needed.

CUSTOMERS

Finally, prioritize what you need most. Do you need deals? Do you need investors? Staff? Tenants? Create your customer personas to represent your customers' wants, needs, and fears. Then get specific in your marketing to attract and engage them.

If it's deals you're after, for example, that needs to become your top priority. The vast majority of your time and attention should go toward networking and finding new deals. Period. But don't waste your time pursuing deals that are not a good fit for your business as it currently is. That is, don't look at portfolios of 500 properties when you know that your first deal is more likely to be 50 units or less.

The same is true of investors, but take the low-hanging fruit if it makes sense for you. Go after the investors who are most likely to give you the money you need. These are investors you already have a relationship or something in common with. And if you're funding your first deal, don't waste your time trying to interest the likes of huge firms like BlackRock. It's highly unlikely they're going to write you a check at this stage.

A key to finding great deals is to establish yourself and build your personal brand in the industry. That's what former law enforcement agent and current CRE firm owner/operator Whitney Sewell did. In 2018, he launched a podcast called *The Real Estate Syndication Show*, despite knowing little about podcasting or about real estate. However, as he interviewed experts for his podcast and researched the industry, he became not only an expert but a recognized expert. The real estate investing podcast took off, and soon he was invited to speak on stages at massive conferences, where he also addressed his support for families looking to adopt children. He then used that very personal aspect of his life to identify and connect with like-minded customers.[5]

His first big deal was in 2019 for $20 million, which required a lot of work despite his growing personal brand. Today, three years later, he can raise that much in a matter of minutes. Whitney's seven-days-a-week podcast is going strong, with more than 1,300 interviews recorded and over 100,000 downloads per month.[6]

The podcast, coupled with his proadoption message, differentiated Whitney and provided a platform to connect with successful real estate pros. His network quickly expanded, thanks to all the time he invested in building the podcast, which then helped his firm grow exponentially.[7]

Whitney started out with no experience and no connections, but leveraged his podcast and his proadoption message to make inroads quickly, growing his CRE venture from $0 to $320 million in three years.[8] That's the power of knowing who your customer is and going after them.

COMMITMENT

Commitment to becoming an innovative, data-driven organization should be front and center in emerging organizations, which already recognize the value data and analytics can provide in becoming a technology company whose product is real estate. This is one area where smaller firms have a distinct advantage, both in recognizing the importance of relying on data and the ability to execute.

Because the organizational chart is smaller, getting everyone on board and in alignment is less challenging, generally, for emerging firms than for major global corporations. Commitment is a big advantage for emerging CRE firms, even if economic and human resources are not as strong.

By applying the innovation framework, you can grow your firm to whatever size you aspire to be. The work you put in should become a constant feedback loop, where the tactics that work generate results that fuel your growth and those that don't fall off your to-do list. Do more of what works and less of what doesn't.

Some folks are happy to stay small, keep their organization lean, and focus on profitability rather than the number of units. For those who want to grow to something larger, the next step up is to become a midmarket firm.

Next steps

The stage of growth your firm is in should determine where your focus is right now. You can download a checklist of what emerging firms should be focusing on here: https://robfinlay.com/books /beyond-the-building.

CHAPTER 8

Midmarket Firms

CONGRATULATIONS ON MAKING IT to the level of a midmarket firm! You've moved beyond being an emerging firm and now you're buying deals, courting large investors, and have built a substantial organization with processes and policies established to guide the firm's operation and growth. You have teams focused on acquisitions, finance, and operations. You've evolved from one or two people buying a few investment properties with your own capital or that of friends and family to a real estate business that has a sophisticated acquisitions and fundraising machine.

Although midmarket firms have evolved from emerging ventures to more established companies, they still have tremendous growth potential. The next step is to scale. To do this, the midmarket firm looks for ways to take the base assets and capabilities they've established and to improve them so they are more effective and efficient.

Although the midmarket is one of the most competitive spaces for CRE operators in the US, firms in this space are in a prime position to take advantage of the opportunities that innovation and data deliver. According to my estimates, in the US alone there are some-where between 10,000 and 25,000 midmarket CRE firms—those that have been in business for at least a few years and which have more than four assets, or between approximately $200 million and up to $2 billion in assets under management. These firms have imple-mented a successful strategy, and all the players are going after the same deals. They're all going after the same investors. And, in many cases, they're going after the same employees. This is where an invest-ment in innovation can truly supercharge your business by giving you an edge over your competition.

INVITING CHANGE

What midmarket firms are also grappling with, on top of growth, is employees who want to continue doing things the way they've always done them. Now that your firm has a successful track record, some employees will use that as proof that things should stay exactly the way they are.

As I mentioned before, according to Deloitte, 60 to 70 percent of broad efforts to introduce change within organizations fail.[1] They fail because humans resist change. It's a natural human tendency to prefer the status quo. But, of course, the more employees fight needed change, improvement, or innovation, the lower your odds of success. These same employees probably recognize the value of change and know that it would result in progress. A willingness to change, to improve, is key at this stage of business growth.

Advocating and managing change is one of the most difficult challenges at a midsize firm. Long-term employees have contributed to the company's success to date and want things to stay the way they are, and newer employees don't have the standing to push for change.

This dynamic is why change is harder to manage in midsize firms with dozens or hundreds of employees than in smaller companies.

Trying to achieve buy-in can sometimes feel like you're herding cats. But that buy-in is essential.

THE INNOVATION FRAMEWORK

Having grown beyond the emerging stage, midmarket companies have the advantage of credibility and enough people to get things done without everyone having to take on several roles. At this stage, a simple framework for innovation and even small investments in staffing technology and operational efficiencies will position you to reap huge returns.

Alan Hammer, partner and executive committee member of the Brach Eichler law firm, is a prime example of how innovation can help a midmarket company be successful. In addition to having spent more than 50 years in law, Alan also runs a midmarket real estate business, having bought his first apartment house—which became his specialty—in 1972. Today, he owns thousands of units.

In law, as in real estate, being able to anticipate what's coming, to plan for several different potentialities, has many advantages. Alan has always been able to see things differently and uses that to his advantage in all aspects of his law and real estate careers.

Early on, he recognized the benefit of buying locally, with a heavy concentration in the suburbs of New York City. The vast majority of his thousands of units are located throughout New Jersey, with the largest being a 480-unit building and the smallest, 20 units. He and his investing partners choose properties based on location, rather than size or other factors.

Alan gathers information from tenants, fellow real estate companies, and investors about what will yield alpha. And then he invests as little as possible in the biggest ROI project. That might be a kitchen overhaul or a bathroom renovation or maybe installing new flooring. He gathers data and then takes action when it is in both his and his tenants' best interests, which maximizes alpha. The operational efficiency—the key innovation—is not the low-cost value-adds that attract and keep good tenants and raise the property value; it's the data that informs Alan's decisions about how to invest in his properties. Alan is a master at low-cost, high-value renovations because of his data-collection techniques.

Is it high tech? Most definitely not. But is it innovative? Absolutely. We all know that the market is going to go through some gyrations in the next few years. There will be adjustments. We can see it coming. As a midmarket firm, with your experience, staff, and connections to funding, you are in a prime position to take advantage of the opportunities that will come. And if you implement the innovation framework, you will be able to capitalize above and beyond the obvious by spotting the trends, and you'll have the organization in place to be able to handle coming changes and profit from them.

LEADERSHIP

Within midmarket firms, typically I speak to the principals and the first layers of senior managers about the innovation framework, with the expectation that they will share the information with their direct reports, who will then help cascade it throughout the organization. To become a technology firm whose product is CRE, the mandate needs to come from the top—from you. It starts with the OKRs and goals that are specific to midmarket firms.

OKRS AND GOALS

At this stage, OKRs are even more critical than they were when your firm was just getting started. When you're small, it's easy to get your team on the same page. Now that you have a larger entity with more people, more effort is required to help everyone within the firm understand what the OKRs are and how important they are to track and achieve.

At this more established stage of development, you should set three OKRs related to the following areas:

- How your brand will set the business apart; what do you do that is different from the thousands of others that do the same?
- Organizational excellence and what that looks like
- Senior team member individual OKRs for their divisions (acquisitions, finance, operations, etc.)

Next, just like in the emerging firm example, you need to create two or three KPIs that tie into each of those three OKRs. Again, you don't have to make this complex, but OKRs are important and need to be set—period. Hire a consultant, use software, or jot them down on paper; it doesn't really matter how you create and record them, as long as you do it.

It's much more important to ensure you've recorded the OKRs your company and senior management are working toward and the individual KPIs you're using to measure your progress than anything else. Keep it simple if you need to, but make sure you're actually tracking your progress. And then go back and review the KPIs at least quarterly. Review the reports on your company's performance, and then adjust your strategy and tactics in order to do more of what works and less of what doesn't. The real value in this process is monitoring the results you're getting, adjusting strategies and tactics to improve performance, and then continuously iterating. This is a feedback loop, really, that is designed to help you constantly level up your results.

EMPLOYEES

As a midmarket company, you must make the investment to hire, train, and enhance your analytics team. You need to enable them to make impactful analyses. If you've decided that your company is going to be data-driven, you have to provide the training to enable employees to do their job to the best of their abilities. That means educating the analyst team so they can create benchmarks and KPIs for all the company's departments

At this stage, you need to have people who are trained data analysts. My recommendation is that 20 percent of all your analysts should be data analysts, at least initially. With their help, you can set KPIs, create plans, and initiate new marketing strategies based on the results they report. Every department relies on data and analytics. You need to enable and empower them so they can better execute on your vision and strategies.

CUSTOMERS

Finally, for each of your customer categories—investors, tenants, employees—develop four or five customer personas each. These are the types of customers and the individual wants, needs, and fears that drive them. Once you've defined all these personas, you're ready to invest more in your marketing to attract customers that are an exact match for your company's focus and capabilities.

Take, for example, Sharif El-Gamal, the chairman and CEO of SOHO Properties, a large Manhattan-based developer and investor in office, retail, hospitality, and residential whose most recent development, Margaritaville Resort Times Square, was named "Best New Hotel" on USA Today's 10 Best Readers' Choice Awards.[2]

Sharif stumbled into real estate 25 years ago and quickly grew a successful development and investment business. After just one year, Sharif was managing a portfolio of valuable properties. However, unknown to him, one of his clients assumed he was Jewish; when he discovered that Sharif was, in fact, Muslim, he fired him. Instead of being crushed, Sharif recognized the opportunity in front of him.[3] "It was one of the best things that ever happened to me," Sharif said, because it pushed him to find and connect with the Muslim community in Manhattan.[4] In zeroing in on members of his own religious community, he quickly evolved from being a broker to establishing himself as a principal investor acquiring properties to own and manage, all by living with integrity and not compromising his values.[5]

What propelled him to the top initially was paying attention to how others were doing business and finding ways to be more creative. Differentiating himself and establishing ethical investment strategies continues to serve him well. By focusing on his identity as a Muslim, Sharif founded what is today a large, well-respected, and recognized real estate development and investment firm headquartered in New York City.

THE POWER OF DATA

Leveraging the data generated by the company, midmarket firms can more easily fine-tune asset management, spot trends in their markets, optimize properties, and increase net operating income. With more historical data and analytics comes the ability to make better-informed decisions. Informed decisions increase net operating income and asset value. That's a huge advantage for a CRE company.

Unlike emerging firms, which have little in the way of resources or internal data, midmarket firms have a track record and a foundation of data that can be used to evaluate what's happening within the company and in the marketplace. Not only can they evaluate the secondary data that nearly everyone has access to, such as published reports or customer data, but they can overlay their own data on top of public data to derive even more useful information.

Of course, relying on any data sources, primary or secondary, is already a step above the intuition and gut feel that some real estate veterans lean on. But, as we all know, intuition is often developed based on past events, and past performance does not necessarily indicate future results or potential. That's the danger of relying on what you've seen in the past to drive future decision-making. The ability to tap into data is what will confirm that intuition or completely refute it. And midmarket firms have the resources, if they choose to apply them, to aggregate, translate, and analyze data to generate useful information.

Data and analytics applied in a midmarket firm is incredibly powerful. Midmarket firms have the opportunity to see around the corner, by leveraging the internal resources they've established and the data they have access to.

Where emerging firms have access to external, public data, which virtually everyone does, they typically don't have resources yet to make that data relevant. That is, they don't have anything to compare it to. For example, they can look at benchmark data for, say, Colorado Springs multifamily units, but without their own property there to benchmark, that data isn't relevant. Or if they can see that the Treasury curve is at a prime point for refinancing but they don't have any loans to refinance, that information is useless. There's no way to act on it or take advantage of it, because emerging firms generally haven't done the deals.

Midmarket firms, in contrast, have plenty of resources. They have properties and people and infrastructure and capital, all of which can be leveraged to make sense of the external data they have access to, as well as the internal data for comparison.

Being able to make sense of data is the difference between knowing that rents went up and knowing what caused it. Were you able to charge more because you spent more money on marketing to drive up demand? Was it because your property manager rented to nicer people, who gave the property higher reviews? Was it because of the money you spent on upgrading the units themselves? Or was it something else, like the new Whole Foods around the corner? Unless you have data and analytics, you have no way of knowing what's behind the higher rents, no way of quantifying the various factors and analyzing their impact.

There is also the data of the organization—the KPIs—for better performance. It's a cycle, really, as shown below.

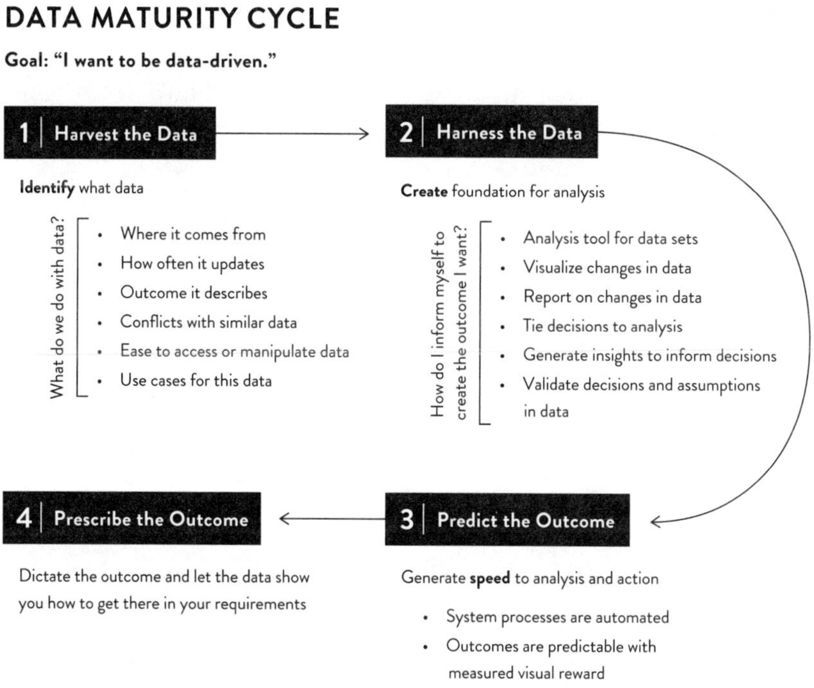

DATA MATURITY CYCLE

Goal: "I want to be data-driven."

Figure 8.1

Midmarket firms take an action, such-as engaging brokers to find and close more deals. The results those brokers achieve can be measured against the KPI—the expected result—to evaluate how they performed. The firm's leaders then make a decision about what needs to be adjusted to improve performance going forward. Then another action is taken, such as creating better relationships with brokers to find more deals or increasing the size of their acquisitions team or building up their investment team, in order to hit those KPIs and get better results. It's a continuous improvement cycle designed to find more alpha by leveraging data.

Next steps

The stage of growth your firm is in should determine where your focus is right now. You can download a checklist of what mid-market firms should focus on here: https://robfinlay.com/books/beyond-the-building.

CHAPTER 9

Corporate Firms

RIGHT NOW, WE'RE SEEING a lot of large corporations pivoting. Facebook has become Meta, DoorDash is expanding from restaurant delivery to household essentials, Walmart is muscling in on Amazon's order delivery model, and numerous print magazines are going 100 percent digital. Those companies that fail to pivot or are unwilling to may face even greater challenges in the future, as technology continues to force change in order to keep up.

CEOs need to be paranoid today to avoid the fate of Blockbuster and Kodak and Kmart. They need to be constantly looking around the corner, to be able to anticipate the looming threats and be able to adapt quickly.

Once again, to reiterate what Sandeep Mathrani, the CEO of WeWork, told me, this resistance to change is caused by arrogance and a lack of properly placed fear. When companies reach a point where they are sure of their continued success, they are doomed. He points out that failing to change and innovate, a major failure of leadership, is a guarantee of failure.[1]

And Sandeep would know, having risen quickly in the ranks of leading real estate companies. Before taking the helm at WeWork in 2020, he was CEO of Brookfield Properties' retail group and was CEO for eight years before that of General Growth Properties, which was purchased by Brookfield in 2018. He served as president of Vornado Realty Trust before that and executive vice president of Forest City Ratner before that.[2] He has developed a reputation for successful turnarounds and business growth.

Through all of his experience, he has led by finding innovative solutions to corporate problems. He has not been afraid to pivot or take the uncommon path in search of success, and I have no doubt he will continue to succeed at WeWork.

My goal here is to help the largest CRE firms gauge how they stack up against their competition, and learn how to apply the principles and practices of innovation in order to come out on top.

GOING BIG

When midmarket firms get to a point in their growth where the company's future is not dictated by a single individual, they've reached the corporate or institutional level. At that point, they have a solid infrastructure with policies and procedures, committees and department heads, and a corporate board guiding the firm's future. The business has evolved to become an organization rather than a group of aligned partners. Decisions at this level are often made through consensus.

A CEO's job is so different today from even a decade ago. We've got diversity, equity, and inclusion; environmental, social, and governance; work from home; and of course side hustles to address. Today, CEOs are expected to be much more compassionate, much more understanding in their treatment of employees. The hardest part for organizations at this level is managing human resources. You may have the financial resources to do everything you want, but achieving alignment among the people in your organization will be nearly impossible. Without agreement on expectations at all levels of the company, growth will be painful. The employees' goals and mission need to align with your company's in order to hold on to them. Leadership is different now.

The problem at this level is that many companies that have been around for decades have long-term employees that have become used to the status quo and see no reason to shake things up. This isn't just an issue with baby boomers anymore. Even younger generations may resist new technology or tools that they perceive as threats to their jobs. When that happens, they might put up roadblocks that can hamper the success of the entire company. That's why I say that the biggest challenge corporations face is their loyal employees.

INNOVATION IS ABOUT THINKING DIFFERENTLY

At the corporate level, managing people becomes your growth driver. Those who aren't willing to change need to be let go. You can't be an innovative company unless you have people who embrace innovation.

At an emerging firm, the president or leader can walk over to talk to their lone employee or to the small team and explain things, get feedback instantly, and make decisions. Bam, it's taken care of. One conversation or meeting is all that's needed to get everyone aligned. But in a corporate environment, there are more layers through which that message needs to be communicated. The distance between senior management and technicians can result in something like the old game of telephone, where the original message gets increasingly muddled as it is conveyed through more layers. Those layers are a corporation's biggest disadvantage.

The CEO needs to share the vision and expectations with their direct reports, who then need to cascade the objective accurately to their direct reports and so on down the line. Unfortunately, by the fifth or sixth sharing of the information, the objective and the excitement surrounding what that means for the organization can be dulled. That's why it can be challenging to achieve alignment through all staffing levels as the organization grows. However, alignment is critical for success at this stage. Once again, OKRs will be one of your best tools, but how you use them in a corporate environment differs in key ways from implementation at emerging and midmarket firms.

At Lobby, we set OKRs at the CEO level and then break them down into expectations at each subsequent reporting layer. We use software called Culture Amp to set and track OKRs, because it would be nearly impossible to manage them on an individual level manually. Different departments have key results they are expected to achieve, based on the corporate goals that have been set, which then leads to specific results that individual workers need to achieve in order to reach the desired goals of the company.

As your company grows, your data consumption and creation expand exponentially, and that means different tools for collecting and managing your data. As a corporation, instead of using a simple tool like an Excel or SQL database, you'll now use a large-scale data warehouse, data ops, and multiple business intelligence systems. As your data usage expands, the tools you need to store and manage it will become more complex and powerful.

AGGRESSIVE TRANSPARENCY

AWH Partners is a privately held real estate investment firm founded by Blackstone Group alums Russell Flicker, Jon Rosenfeld, and Chad Cooley. The firm has invested more than $2 billion in hotel real estate in partnership with marquis institutional capital providers and global investors. Part of its success strategy involves "aggressive transparency," Russ explains[3]—building credibility and closer relationships with their investors by never sugarcoating bad news. In fact, they lead with any negative information, often emphasizing the worst possible outcome so that investors are never caught off guard. Fortunately, they rarely have negative news to share.[4]

Technology is key to AWH Partners' ability to be transparent. Technology has made it possible to capture years of data from thousands of hotels across the US. Not only can AWH Partners share up-to-date information with investors and prove they know what they're doing, but the data helps them find the best deals, like underperforming hotels they can turn around. Data also helps them improve the hotels they already own.[5]

The founders realized early on that data and analytics were imperative to the company's success. Not only does data enable them to act quickly on deals, but it also makes it possible to break down silos and enables teams to work better together.[6]

Although AWH Partners is a large corporate enterprise, it can act like a nimble emerging firm by gathering, managing, analyzing, and sharing its data throughout the entire organization. Technology and data allow them to be transparent both internally and externally. That gives them tremendous potential for innovation and success.[7]

A WORD OF CAUTION

For those of you who run a corporate firm, I'm sure you already have big data and analytics tech in place and that you're putting it to work within your organization. To get to multiple billions of dollars in market cap, you have to. And I'll bet your company is generating lots of data, but my follow-up question is this: What are you doing with it? What does your feedback loop look like, in order to effect change based on all that data? How do you make sure you're tapping into that data to get you to the front, help you continue to think differently once you're there, and keep you out front?

As a larger company, you're going to have data ops, data validations, different data systems, a data warehouse, dev ops, and the human resources required to make sense of all the data your business is generating and storing. Your team will include data analysts, business intelligence analysts, and maybe even data scientists.

Despite all this infrastructure, the good news is that your return on data and analytics will be even higher than those of smaller CRE firms. It's the benefit of economies of scale, really. For example, if you have 500 properties and thousands of people on your payroll who are supported by tech tools, you've generated a massive amount of data on a daily basis just through the normal course of doing business. That data can be mined for insights a smaller firm simply wouldn't have access to.

My word of warning at this stage, however, is not to get too big for your britches. Stay humble. Be paranoid. If you continue to do business the way you've always done it, you won't remain in business. There are thousands of firms behind you that are looking to move up and take your place.

Next steps

The stage of growth your firm is in should determine where your focus is right now. You can download a checklist of what corporate firms should be focusing on here: https://robfinlay.com/books /beyond-the-building.

CHAPTER 10

Iteration

CONTINUOUS INNOVATION AND EVOLUTION are the keys to success in technology companies whose product is CRE. Whether that innovation is technology driven matters less than the constant adjusting and adapting that needs to occur.

There's no other CRE professional I can think of who has done that better than my father, Christopher Finlay. He owns and runs the Lloyd Jones companies, which are focused on multifamily and senior housing investment, development, and management. My dad was extremely successful in his career. He actually began as an airline pilot with Eastern Airlines. During this time, he invested in real estate on the side, but his side business quickly evolved into a full-time career growing a major CRE operation. In 1983, he left Eastern to concentrate 100 percent on his CRE ventures.

He has been so successful because he is always willing to iterate or pivot, depending on what's going on in the market. Over the past 40 years, the market has experienced many ups and downs, including five recessions. I don't know anyone who has had the courage to pivot as many times as he has, based on what he could see coming around the corner. He is able to view real estate from a 50,000-foot view, taking in the whole, rather than zeroing in too closely on specific categories. That has meant that he has invested in and built post offices, senior housing, and market-rate and tax-credit housing; he has started brokerage, property management, and construction businesses because he understands the importance of not pigeonholing yourself or your company into one category. He has always maintained the flexibility to react to changing markets. He is always evolving, relying on data to make informed decisions, and ensuring that decisions by others in the company are data-driven as well.

Having always been a technology early adopter (I was the first kid in town to have a phone in my family car!), he is basically his own data and analytics team. He has always been a voracious reader, devouring hundreds of books, articles, and papers on every topic imaginable on a regular basis. On top of that, he regularly attends industry trade shows and conferences and is always taking online classes. He is driven by data gathering on a personal level; he always has been. That drive has enabled him to build enterprise value in every company he's ever created. But individuals and companies are different.

At a firm level, becoming data-driven and innovative isn't something that happens in one fell swoop. It's an ongoing process of continuous improvement. In order to stay ahead of the pack, you need to constantly refer back to the data. What is it telling you about the market, your tenants, investors, and your own operations? The process of becoming an innovative and data-driven enterprise is iterative. It is ever changing, and if you don't at least try to keep up, you will be left in the dust.

My hope is that this book provides a framework for you to use on a regular basis so you can get ahead and stay ahead of the competition. Conversely, if you stop paying attention to your data, you'll lose any advantage you've amassed.

As your business evolves, understand that you'll need to make changes within its various parts. You'll need to upgrade your technology, for example, as well as your internal systems, by leveraging your economic resources and your human resources. Some employees' commitment to becoming data-centric may wane, and you need to be prepared for that and be willing to hire people who are more adaptable.

The technology, processes, and people you have today may not be what you need to move you closer to your goals. Some of those elements are able to grow and adapt, and some are not. Only you can decide when you've hit a roadblock in one of those areas that needs to be cleared through the application of your economic resources, human resources, and commitment.

FOSTERING INNOVATION BEGINS WITH A WILLINGNESS TO CHANGE

Plenty of business leaders will claim to be willing to innovate, and they talk about how they foster change within their organizations, but they won't listen to other opinions about it. In truth, they're not open to change or to innovation.

Anyone who has a securitized loan has probably dealt with SitusAMC. With 7,000 employees at 38 domestic and international offices, SitusAMC is a CRE powerhouse.[1] But that wasn't always the case. Twenty-five-plus years ago, I met Steve Powel, Martin Bronstein, and Ralph Howard—the original partners in Situs. At the time, they had a small contract commercial loan underwriting and financial due diligence shop. Most securitized, aka Wall Street, lenders do not actually do the underwriting of the loans. Instead, they subcontract to these underwriters.[2] Third-party underwriting and due diligence are a tough business because most view them as a commodity. How do you differentiate yourself from others who do the same exact thing? How do you create enterprise value, because scaling just means hiring more underwriters? And how do you identify business opportunities when you just look at deals, underwrite them, close them, and move on to the next?

How Situs grew from three guys running around at conferences pitching their wares in the early '90s to one of the largest global financial services and technology firms in the commercial and residential mortgage industries can be summed up in one word: innovation. They just did things differently. They were not afraid to try new things that other firms would never do, like technology adoption, data aggregation, robotic automation, and artificial intelligence.[3]

By leveraging relationships, taking changes, and making investments in their people, processes, and technology, they created enterprise value. They started spotting trends. By maintaining the connection point with the loans that they were underwriting through servicing and asset management, they created a continuous loop of information that enabled them to spot opportunities and trends. Unlike other underwriting and due diligence shops that were involved in the first steps of a financing process, Situs was then helping with the underwriting, the securitization, and the final servicing through asset management. They were involved from the beginning through the middle to the end.[4]

With a commitment to excellence and innovation that differentiated the firm from the very beginning, Situs (now known as SitusAMC) continues its investment in people and technology to maintain its leadership position in the mortgage lending space.[5]

THE NAME OF THE GAME IS DIFFERENTIATION

Change can be overwhelming and daunting, which is why many organizations shy away from it. Change causes upheaval, and few people want that. They generally want the status quo. After all, it's much easier to maintain the status quo than it is to initiate radical change.

Sometimes it's hard to justify change when you aren't aware of how you stack up against the competition. If you think you're doing just fine, you're going to be much less likely to want to change anything, to innovate. To determine how competitive your company is, a good place to start is to do some simple competitive research. That can be as easy as talking to salespeople at other companies to gauge how effective they are at selling. Or you can take a look at the dozens of sales pitches you get on LinkedIn to see what they're selling and how effective their pitch is. You could also go to real estate industry conferences and take time to size up your competition all in one place.

Our company is constantly conducting competitive analyses to see what's going on in the marketplace and determine where we currently fit. CRE organizations generally do a good job of comparing properties, of creating competitive sets at that level. But, as I've said before, too few CRE companies put together competitive sets to see where they're strong and where they may be weak *at the organizational level*.

There are also steps you can take to encourage innovation at the organizational level. For example, you could set up an internal innovation committee composed of members of different departments who meet regularly to share what they've witnessed in the industry, what new challenges are appearing, and possible solutions or new technology. Tapping into new and different sources of information can be enough to open your company up to new opportunities or, at least, to be able to spot them.

The dynamics of where and how we consume information continues to change. The print newspaper used to be the primary source of news years ago, and then TV became important until the rise of the internet attracted users online for timely information. Once there, people frequently turned to blogs for up-to-date news, and now social media has become more important as an information source. Not too far in the future, our information sources will likely be something else, either a different platform or a different format.

Being open to receiving information from new channels significantly increases the opportunities for change and for innovation. Seek out new data sources, consider how what you're hearing fits with what you already know, and then look for patterns within the new information you're gathering.

LinkedIn can be a good source of competitive information to see what salespeople in your industry are trying to sell you. It can also be an effective marketing tool. For example, although it is not in the CRE space, software developer Chili Piper is using its LinkedIn company page to raise brand awareness by hosting competitions highlighting people who are their ideal customer and asking their target audience to vote on which candidate should win a grand prize. That one tactic earned them 10,000 new subscribers in one month.[6]

Another LinkedIn success story is defense contractor L3Harris, which wanted to get a new product in front of a specific Air Force general. But instead of using the company's LinkedIn page, the marketing team made posts on the president's profile page, followed by a commenting campaign that earned those posts hundreds of thousands of views and a private call with their target general. It would be easy for CRE firms to adopt similar marketing tactics, to pursue joint venture partners or investors, or to get plugged in to industry happenings.

Another way to develop the skill of recognizing patterns and new opportunities is to constantly ask yourself, "How would I do this differently?" Practice asking this question regularly, to train your brain to recognize new ways to apply what you already know. For example, last week I used the Jersey Mike's app to order my favorite sub, and while I was waiting for it, I began to ask myself how I would change the order process, how I would change the production process, the store design, the app design. Pushing yourself to spot improvement opportunities is the key to being able to see around the corner (although I love Jersey Mike's and the app just the way it is and would do little to change the experience).

By studying how other companies do business and breaking the customer experience down into its individual parts, you can then consider how you might take those observations and apply them to your own business. Recognizing the great experience you had at another company, how could you do something similar on your own to improve *your* customer's experience? Conversely, how can you ensure that your customers never have to go through the terrible experience you just had in dealing with one of your contractors, for example?

That's essentially what continuous innovation consists of—paying attention to what's going on around you and considering what the impact might be. What challenges are emerging? What new technology tools are being developed to address them? How are they working? What's still needed?

Besides paying attention to the data, innovators need to be fearful, says WeWork's Sandeep Mathrani. Citing example after example of companies that are extinct because they could not adapt, Sandeep says the key is feeling fear—of never becoming complacent or arrogant.[7] He points to businesses like Kmart, Blockbuster, Blackberry, Sears, and AOL as companies that didn't pay attention to what was going on around them or, at least, didn't believe they could fail. But they did. They are obsolete because they were so sure they couldn't be better, and their competitors passed them by.[8]

People think that innovation needs to be something that changes the world, but it doesn't. Some of the best innovations are iterations or evolutions rather than radical revolutions. Iterative improvements add up.

WHAT'S YOUR EXIT STRATEGY?

By following the advice in this book, you should now have some ideas for how to differentiate your firm for equity and equity players by creating enterprise value and spotting opportunities and trends in the market. What comes next?

Every one of us will make an exit, but not all of us have a strategy for what happens when we do. Unfortunately, those who fail to make a plan often end up at the mercy of others who may not have your best interests at heart.

There are three basic types of exits for CRE owners:

- Sell your business
- Go public
- Transfer it to your kids

There's a fourth type of exit—going out of business—but I'll assume you don't plan on using that one.

I can't tell you which exit is the right one for you, nor the right strategy to put in place to execute it effectively. What I can say with 100 percent certainty is that any strategy is better than no strategy at all.

The right strategy for now may be to keep your options open, but that doesn't mean doing nothing. Instead, it means preparing for every option so that you can pick and choose the best one at the best time.

Next steps

No one person could create the kind of structures we build today, whether it's a magnificent skyscraper, complex logistics warehouse, or relatively simple self-storage facility. The expertise was accumulated over time—one small innovation after another, a spark of genius here, a straightforward improvement there.

I've built CRE companies worth hundreds of millions, but I didn't do it by myself. My family got me started and gave me my foundation. The jobs I worked in connected me with great mentors. Partners helped me start and grow my own businesses.

In this book, I've tried to condense and share the principles, tools, and practices that have been most valuable to me. I hope by sharing them with you, you can take your existing business to new heights or build something completely novel that surprises us all.

I'd love to hear how you've implemented the strategies shared in this book, and any suggestions you feel would improve a future version. Please visit RobFinlay.com and tell me about your successes!

Acknowledgments

FOR THE EXPERIENCE, KNOWLEDGE, and ideas in this book, I owe not only my family, who got me started in real estate, but also friends, business partners, coworkers, clients, and associates—too many to mention, although I will thank as many as I can and apologize to anyone I've inadvertently left out. Many thanks to Mike Altman, Justin Nonemaker, Eric Zagorsky, Willy Walker, Sandeep Mathrani, Peter Slaugh, Joe Lubeck, Steve Katz, Michael Episcope, Brady Sullivan, Max Bresner, Whitney Sewell, Alan Hammer, Sharif El-Gamal, Russ Flicker, Chris Finlay, Steve Powel, Kevin Swill, Anne Hollander, and Amanda Kuehl.

Special thanks goes to Dan Monfried, who spent countless hours challenging my ideas and giving me new ones to think about, editing this manuscript, and assisting me with research.

Beyond the Building is infinitely better because of all of you.

Appendix

HEAD OF ENGAGEMENT

Job Summary

We are looking for a head of engagement who will be responsible for creating and maintaining customer relationships for the company. This person will need to understand the personas of our customers to develop strategic initiatives focused on acquiring new customers while also engaging our current customers. The head of engagement will ensure all channels of the company are aligned so we are efficiently targeting our customers' wants and needs.

Responsibilities

- Identify all customers and customer personas in the organization, including our tenants, investors, employees, and others that help drive business value.

- Establish tools, processes, and systems that drive customer engagement while also targeting new customers.
- Create strategies, specifically tying back to customers and customer personas, to leverage the customers' wants and needs to drive engagement.
- Develop marketing and sales initiatives to target new customers and drive revenue.
- Cultivate initiatives to track the current engagement of our customers.
- Prepare key performance indicators (KPIs) to track effectiveness of our customers' engagement.

Requirements

- Hands-on attitude, with the ability to lead and effectively manage resources
- Detail-oriented self-starter with strong execution, problem-solving, and follow-up skills
- Ability to foster strong relationships and inspire, motivate, and nurture them
- Proven track record for managing, owning, and optimizing high-impact projects/processes
- Comfort in trying new things, testing hypotheses, and adapting quickly
- Excellent verbal and written communication skills
- Demonstrated analytical skills
- Bachelor's degree in business, communications, or a related field; MBA preferred

REAL ESTATE DATA ANALYST

Job Summary

Seeking a real estate data analyst who will be responsible for real estate data management and analysis.

The analyst will work on the creation and analysis of financial models and industry- and market-specific research, and present the findings to internal and external stakeholders. The analyst will assist with acquisition underwriting, financial due diligence, and post-closing asset monitoring for the portfolio of properties.

The analyst will work closely with senior team members on the debt and equity deal structure and cash flow waterfall modeling. The analyst will be responsible for modeling quarterly asset valuations, sale/refi scenarios, and monthly property and financial performance to GP and LP Investors.

The analyst will be responsible for tracking and reporting performance metrics and developing predictive analytics across the portfolio.

The analyst will be responsible for receipt, validation, cleaning, and storage of the source data. Post receipt, the data will be normalized and stored in groups of data that are then shared and visualized into consumable BI dashboards. These dashboards will be the performance metrics used by operational, sales, and marketing teams for measuring against the company objectives.

The analyst will have exposure to private and institutional real estate owners and operators. Internally, they will work closely with property managers, asset managers, portfolio managers, accounting and finance teams.

Required skills include accounting, modeling, corporate finance, underwriting, and financial analysis. The analyst will need to utilize scripts language (like Python and R) to perform predictive analytics. Additional internal and external data sets will continue to be incorporated as the company looks to leverage more data-driven decision-making across the portfolio.

Responsibilities

- Work on modeling property acquisitions and dispositions.
- Work directly with the portfolio management team on weekly and monthly property and portfolio performance reports along with comparison analysis to budget and proformas.
- Analyze external market data across multiple property types and data sources.
- Identify discrepancies and defects, alert teams of issues, troubleshoot and implement corrective actions, and improve auditing capabilities.
- Collaborate with modeling team to perform data validations and data model changes.
- Work with C-level executives to define and track performance across the business to drive strategic decision-making.
- Work with key stakeholders across each vertical to develop measurement frameworks for easily consumable BI dashboards that inform operational, sales, and marketing objectives.
- Schedule ongoing data ingestion to ensure up-to-date reporting. Investigate discrepancies.
- Use scripting languages (like Python and R) to query data and create predictive analytics.

Requirements

- Deadline-focused with strong attention to detail
- Experience working in a fast-paced and dynamic environment with a constantly changing workload, comprising short-term, long-term, and ad hoc projects

- Knowledge of 3rd party data sources CoStar, REIS, and Axiometrics
- Knowledge of ARGUS Enterprise financial modeling
- Knowledge of property management systems, including Yardi, RealPage, Appfolio, MRI, Entrata, ResMan, Rent Manager, etc.
- High-level competency in financial modeling using Excel and VBA
- Proven SQL experience with the ability to write complex queries from relational databases and combine data from multiple data sources
- Strong data management skills, such as transforming raw data files, data cleaning, and handling missing values
- Experience working with databases and data analysis tools
- Experience developing data visualizations with BI tools (Looker, Tableau, etc.)
- Experience with scripting languages (Python, R, etc.)
- Ability to distill complex analyses into simple, easily digestible concepts
- Proven ability to solve complex, analytical problems using quantitative approaches with a blend of analytical and technical skills
- Prior ETL or FTP experience is a plus
- Bachelor's degree in computer science, math, data science, accounting, or equivalent experience

Notes

Chapter 1

1. Tim Stobierski, "The Advantages of Data-Driven Decision-Making," *Harvard Business School Online's Business Insights*, August 26, 2019, https://online.hbs .edu/blog/post/data-driven-decision-making.

Chapter 2

1. "Walker & Dunlop Structures the Sale and Financing for Trails at Timberline in Colorado," Walker & Dunlop Press Releases, October 31, 2022, https://www .walkerdunlop.com/news-and-events/2022-10-31-walker-dunlop-structures-the -sale-and-financing-for-trails-at-timberline-in-colorado.

2. Willy Walker, email to author, July 18, 2022.

3. "Walker & Dunlop, Inc. (WD)," Stock Analysis, accessed March 31, 2022, https:// stockanalysis.com/stocks/wd/market-cap.

4. "Awards & Rankings," Walker & Dunlop, accessed November 14, 2022, https:// www.walkerdunlop.com/what-makes-us-different/awards-and-financial-rankings.

5. Paul Bubny, "One on One with Walker & Dunlop's Willy Walker," *Connect CRE*, October 30, 2019, https://www.connectcre.com/stories/one-on-one-with-walker -dunlops-willy-walker.

6. "Walker & Dunlop Closes GeoPhy Acquisition," Walker & Dunlop Press Releases, February 28, 2022, https://www.walkerdunlop.com/news-and -events/2022-02-28-walker-dunlop-closes-geophy-acquisition.

7. Jon Banister, "A 'Competitive Furnace' Burns Inside Willy Walker," *Bisnow*, May 21, 2020, www.bisnow.com/national/news/capital-markets/the-making-of-willy -walker-104527.

8. Andrew S. Grove, *Only the Paranoid Survive: How to Exploit the Crisis Points That Challenge Every Company* (New York: Currency, 2010).

9. Jim Bright, "What Do 1 in 3 People Say about Change? Some Surprising Stats!," LinkedIn, January 30, 2015, www.linkedin.com/pulse/what-do-1-3-people-say -change-some-surprising-stats-jim-bright.

10. Michael Distefano, "Alan Mulally: The Man Who Saved Ford," Korn Ferry, August 10, 2014, www.kornferry.com/insights/briefings-magazine/issue-20/alan -mulally-man-who-saved-ford.

Chapter 3

1. United States Securities and Exchange Commission, "Mondelēz International, Inc.," February 7, 2020, https://ir.mondelezinternational.com/static-files/e205c4cb -8d44-4449-b213-f0765e3a6301.

2. "Mondelēz Sees eCommerce Growth but Downplays Role of D2C," PYMNTS, January 28, 2022, https://www.pymnts.com/earnings/2022/mondelez-sees -ecommerce-growth-downplays-direct-to-consumer.

3. Mondelēz International, "Mondelēz International Reports Q4 and FY 2020 Results," January 28, 2021, https://ir.mondelezinternational.com/news-releases /news-release-details/mondelez-international-reports-q4-and-fy-2020-results.

4. Mondelēz International, "Mondelēz International Reports Q4 and FY 2021 Results," January 27, 2022, https://ir.mondelezinternational.com/news-releases /news-release-details/mondelez-international-reports-q4-and-fy-2021-results.

5. Harold Geneen with Alvin Moscow, *Managing* (New York: Doubleday, 1984).

6. Kenneth N. Gilpin, "Harold S. Geneen, 87, Dies; Nurtured ITT," *The New York Times*, November 23, 1997, https://www.nytimes.com/1997/11/23/business /harold-s-geneen-87-dies-nurtured-itt.html.

7. Harold Geneen, "The Essential Elements," in *The Book of Management Wisdom: Classic Writings by Legendary Managers*, ed. Peter Krass (New York: Wiley, 2000), 3–6.

8. Gilpin, "Harold S. Geneen, 87, Dies."

9. Gilpin, "Harold S. Geneen, 87, Dies."

10. Gilpin, "Harold S. Geneen, 87, Dies."

11. "Elon Musk," Tesla, accessed November 9, 2022, https://www.tesla.com/elon-musk.

12. U.S. Securities and Exchange Commission, "Tesla Motors Reports First Quarter 2011 Results: Strong Quarterly Revenue and Gross Margin Model S Program Remains on Track for Mid-2012 Deliveries," May 4, 2011, https://www.sec.gov /Archives/edgar/data/1318605/000119312511126139/dex991.htm.

13. Ingvar Kamprad, "The IKEA Vision and Values," IKEA, accessed November 9, 2022, https://www.ikea.com/gb/en/this-is-ikea/about-us/the-ikea-vision-and-values -pub9aa779d0#.

14. Kamprad, "The IKEA Vision and Values."

15. "Amazon Jobs," Amazon, accessed November 9, 2022, https://www.amazon .jobs/en.

16. Mission Statement Academy, "Amazon Mission and Vision Statement Analysis," accessed November 21, 2022, https://mission-statement.com/amazon.

Chapter 4

1. Provided to author by OpenPath, 2022.
2. Joe Lubeck, email to author, July 18, 2022.
3. Lubeck, email.
4. Lubeck, email.
5. Lubeck, email.
6. Lubeck, email.
7. Lubeck, email.

Chapter 5

1. Surabhi Kejriwal, "Gaming the Commercial Real Estate Talent Conundrum: Talent Strategy in a Post-Pandemic World," Deloitte, February 5, 2021, https://www2.deloitte.com/ce/en/pages/real-estate/articles/commercial-real-estate-talent-conundrum-predictions.html.
2. Kateryna Zhukovina, "Commercial Real Estate Data Analytics: Where to Get It?," Ascendix, July 22, 2022, https://ascendix.com/blog/commercial-real-estate-data-analytics.
3. Blackstone, "Data Science," 2022, https://www.blackstone.com/data-science.
4. Capital One, "Pick Me First," accessed November 9, 2022, https://www.ispot.tv/ad/bDQm/capital-one-banking-pick-me-first-featuring-charles-barkley.

Chapter 6

1. Association of National Advertisers, "2022 ANA Response Rate Report—The Results Are In," ANA Event Recaps, October 4, 2022, https://www.ana.net/miccontent/show/id/er-2022-10-mdt-oct22-demand-metric.

Chapter 7

1. Max Bresner, email to author, July 21, 2022.
2. Bresner, email.
3. Beth Archie, "Do Your Employees Resist Change? Here's Why That's a Good Sign," *Spark*, November 30, 2017, www.adp.com/spark/articles/2017/11/do-your-employees-resist-change-heres-why-thats-a-good-sign.aspx.
4. Bresner, email.
5. Whitney Sewell, email to author, July 19, 2022.
6. Sewell, email.
7. Sewell, email.
8. Sewell, email.

Chapter 8

1. Archie, "Do Your Employees Resist Change?"
2. *"Margaritaville Resort Times Square Named 'Best New Hotel' in USA Today's 10 Best Readers' Choice Awards," Cision PR Newswire*, January 4, 2022, https:// www.prnewswire.com/news-releases/margaritaville-resort-times-square-named -best-new-hotel-in-usa-todays-10best-readers-choice-awards-301453662.html; Sharif El-Gamal, email to the author, July 21, 2022.
3. El-Gamal, email.
4. El-Gamal, email.
5. El-Gamal, email.

Chapter 9

1. Sandeep Mathrani, email to author, June 13, 2022.
2. Mathrani, email.
3. Russell Flicker, email to author, July 14, 2022.
4. Flicker, email.
5. Flicker, email.
6. Flicker, email.
7. Flicker, email.

Chapter 10

1. "About Us," SitusAMC, accessed November 28, 2022, https://www.situsamc .com/about-us.
2. Steve Powel, email to author, July 19, 2022.
3. Powel, email.
4. Powel, email.
5. Powel, email.
6. Chili Piper, email to author, December 6, 2022.
7. Sandeep Mathrani, email to author, June 13, 2022.
8. Mathrani, email.

Index

data analysts, 72–73
midmarket firms, 108
Sterling Properties, 75–77
transparency
  aggressive transparency policy,
    116–17
  Origin Investments, 85
troubleshooting
  competitive analyses, 123
  KPIs as tool for, 65
  SWOT analysis, 98

U

Uber, 15
underwriting and due diligence, 17,
  121–22
urban village, 59–61

V

vision and mission statements
  Amazon, 50

IKEA, 49
importance of, 35–36
objectives and key results, 48–50
Tesla, 49

W

Walker & Dunlop, 27–28, 30, 31
Walker Webcasts, 28
Walker, Willy, 27–30, 32
Walmart, 113
weather and leasing data, 16

Z

Zagorsky, Eric, 23
Zuckerman, Wayne, 76

About the Author

ROBERT J. FINLAY, CPM, has launched and sold many successful commercial real estate (CRE) tech and finance startups over the last 20 years, including Commercial Defeasance, Investor Management Services (IMS), and Tax Credit Asset Management (TCAM). Commercial Defeasance was sold to Summit Partners in 2006 (reacquired in 2018), TCAM to MRI Software in 2018, and IMS to RealPage in 2019.

In addition to his entrepreneurial passion and ventures, Finlay owns and operates a substantial portfolio of multifamily and commercial properties as well as securitized debt instruments. He is the chairman and CEO of Thirty Capital, a robust organization serving midmarket CRE management, investment, and private equity firms with technology, finance advisory, and debt management services.

Finlay's inspiration springs from bringing services to market that are ahead of their time, solving real challenges for CRE operators and investors, and creating measurable value. He develops bespoke technologies and services that support and enable optimal efficiency and profitability for commercial real estate investors' operations and ventures. Developing and marketing new technology entails influencing the behavior, expectations, and growth of the CRE industry, and Finlay thrives on a trajectory of service ideation, market entry, brand positioning, and early adoption.

Thirty Capital's software technology and financial advisory services portfolio includes Lobby CRE, EntityKeeper, Thirty Capital Financial, Thirty Capital Performance Group, Thirty Capital Ventures, The Academy of CRE Finance and Innovation, and other ventures. These pioneering enterprises integrate modern technology with expert services to propel the commercial real estate industry's advancement.

Finlay graduated from New Hampshire College with a BS in finance, leading to an early career in financial services on Wall Street with Credit Suisse First Boston and Lehman Brothers. He earned his Certified Property Manager (CPM) certification from the Institute of Real Estate Management in 2019.